KT-167-459

THE BEST
BOOK OF
TRICKS

Ever!

This is a Carlton Book

Text, illustration and design copyright © 1998
Carlton Books Limited

First published 1998 by Carlton Books
Limited, 20 Mortimer Street,
London W1T 3JW

Reprinted 2002

This book is sold subject to the condition that it
shall not, by way of trade or otherwise, be lent,
resold, hired out or otherwise circulated without
the publisher's prior written consent in any form
of cover or binding other than that in which it is
published and without a similar condition including
this condition, being imposed upon the
subsequent purchaser.

All rights reserved.

ISBN 1 85868 479 X

Design and illustration: Giles Ellis

Printed and bound in Great Britain

THE BEST
BOOK OF
TRICKS
Ever!

Compiled by Geoff Tibballs

CARLTON

CONTENTS

Chapter One
Many ways to annoy your friends and humiliate your enemies.

Chapter Two
Become the local card sharp with the simple-but-effective tricks in this chapter.

Chapter Three
Everything you need to show off at your local and impress everyone by juggling your change, pushing glasses through beer mats or even turning water into wine.

Chapter Four
The best of the rest – tricks to perform any time and with the objects you find around you at home, at work or even in the queue at the Post Office.

INTRODUCTION

Within these pages, you will find over 250 tricks, ranging from simple tricks with playing cards and everyday objects to cunning practical jokes. The beauty of the tricks is that anyone can perform them – there are no grand illusions with complicated, expensive equipment.

There are tricks for every occasion – for the kitchen, at work or even in the bank queue. Other tricks are tailored for the pub where you can baffle your friends with your skill at doing unnatural things with ice cubes, beer mats and small change. In addition, there are classical practical jokes for everyone. The key to success with practical jokes is the timing. A hand rising up mysteriously out of the ground may appear hilarious after an all-night party, but may be received with less enthusiasm at a funeral. The best practical jokes should cause an embarrassment which can be overcome by means other than an extensive course of therapy. It is important to choose the right victim – someone with a good sense of humour rather than a person who reacts to any setback by roaming the streets wielding an axe.

To help you choose the tricks best suited to your abilities, each is numbered with a Skill Level from 1 to 10. The higher the number, the more difficult the trick. Similarly the practical jokes are given an Embarrassment Factor of 1 to 10.

Have fun!

Practical jokes and tricks can be dangerous and have serious consequences.

The inclusion of a joke or trick in this book should not be considered recommendation for its use. In undertaking any tricks you should think carefully about potential dangers.

Every effort has been taken to ensure the accuracy and completeness of the information given in this book. No liability can be accepted by the author or the publisher for any loss or damage howsoever caused.

Chapter One:

Practical Jokes and Tricks

The Inverted Matchbox

Skill Level: ❶
Embarrassment Factor: ❹

Practical jokes comes in all shapes and sizes. Some operate on the grand scale and require the sort of elaborate planning which used to be the preserve of shows like "Candid Camera" and "Beadle's About". With others, the charm is in their simplicity. This prank falls into the second category. Choose a victim who is a smoker and wait for him to leave the room for a while. He will invariably leave his box of matches lying on the table. In his absence, swap the box around so that the closed side of the tray is now on the same side as the picture. Leave the box picture-side up for his return so that he won't suspect anything. Then when he comes to open the box, all the matches will fall out on the floor. This spectacle can cause far greater embarrassment if timed to occur at an important business meeting, but your motives might be open to question.

Lager Shower

Skill Level: ❶
Embarrassment Factor: ❹

Certain customs go with certain drinks. Fine wine is swilled lovingly around the palate, dry martini is shaken but not stirred and meths is accompanied by three choruses of "I Belong to Glasgow". Canned lager is shaken so vigorously that whoever opens it is covered in a sea of foam. As with everything, the timing is crucial. If at all possible, you should hand your friend the shaken can so that the grand opening coincides with him attempting to chat up the girl you fancy. By the time he has gone to clean himself up, you will have moved in. Even if he decides to press on regardless, the chances are she won't want to get too close to someone who stinks like a brewery, unless of course she's got a part-time job as a shire horse.

Say It With Flowers

Skill Level: ❶
Embarrassment Factor: ❿

Warning: This trick could be dangerous. Take care!

If you don't mind spending money in your eternal quest to embarrass your friends, an outlay of about £10 can secure you a potential marriage-wrecker! But make sure that it is a friend on whom you play this trick, so that you can patch things up afterwards. You need to wait until your friend has spent a few days away alone – perhaps a business trip or the UK Solitaire Championships – and on his return, send him a big bunch of flowers with a romantic message on the card. Time the flowers to arrive when you're certain that his other half will be at home so that he can't bury them at the bottom of the dustbin and pretend they never arrived. If you're a real sadist, you could casually drop by that evening so that you can witness the mayhem you've caused, but there's always the danger that your expression might give the game away too quickly. Besides, his mood the next time you talk to him will be a sure sign as to whether your plot has had the desired effect. If the acrimony lingers, you will need to own up, preferably before solicitors become involved.

Hide and Don't Seek

Skill Level: ❷
Embarrassment Factor: ❺

Ever since the news story about the Irish hide and seek champion being found dead in a cupboard, this age-old pastime has been deemed too dangerous for some households, but it can still be incorporated into a cruel practical joke. When the evening is really going with a thud, you've run out of lager, there's no football on the telly and the only video left to watch is of your sister giving birth, why not suggest a game of hide and seek? One person will be unbearably enthusiastic, insisting that he knows a place where none of you will ever find him. So you tell him to go and hide and then you all disappear down to the pub. By the time he realizes he's been tricked, it will be his round.

Catch The Egg

 **Skill Level:** ❷
Embarrassment Factor: ❼

YOU WILL NEED:
AN EGG, A BALL

Eggs are very versatile, not least because there are so many practical jokes you can play with them. One of the easiest – and messiest – involves secretly substituting an egg for a ball during a game of catch. On summer afternoons, parks are full of groups of lads trying to offset their steady diet of lager and fast food with a spot of healthy exercise. For some, this entails nothing more than a few arm jerks in recognition of a passing girl, but for the more energetic it could entail kicking around a football, an impromptu game of cricket or volleyball, hurling a frisbee or simply throwing a tennis ball among themselves. Unless you are confident of your ability to make an omelette impersonate a frisbee, the egg substitution trick is best performed with a tennis ball. It is most effective when there three or four of you playing. Keep the egg in your pocket for the first few rounds so that you have all built up to a point where you are throwing and catching at speed. At an opportune moment, bring the egg into your left hand. As you catch the ball right-handed, quickly switch egg and ball and toss the egg to the next catcher. By now, he will be operating on automatic pilot and probably won't notice anything out of the ordinary about the projectile hurtling towards him. Even if he does spot that it's an egg, his natural instinct will still be to catch it. Either way, it will make an unholy mess as it splatters into his hands.

Minefield

 **Skill Level:** ❷
Embarrassment Factor: ❸

YOU WILL NEED:
SIX PLATES, A BLINDFOLD

This is a daft trick for parties. Suggest a game of "Minefield" and scatter half a dozen plates around the floor. Tell the contestant that each plate represents a landmine which, for obvious reasons, he must avoid. But then having blindfolded him, you secretly remove the plates, leaving him prancing around like a demented hop-scotch dancer trying to steer clear of imaginary obstacles. Prolong the agony for as long as possible with cries of "Look out", "Mind that one" etc. When his legs are about to drop off through exhaustion, remove the blindfold and let him realize what a fool he's been made to look.

The Thin Black Line

Skill Level: ❷
Embarrassment Factor: ❹

YOU WILL NEED:
A COIN, A PENCIL, A PIECE OF PAPER

Sometimes it seems unfair to take advantage of the extremely gullible or the extremely drunk, but there are occasions when you just have to abandon such lofty principles. This is one such instance. Tell your victim that you're going to make his hand really giddy and then see whether he can roll a coin down his nose. In the misplaced belief that he is neither stupid nor drunk, he will accept the challenge with relish. Place the coin on a sheet of paper and ask him to draw round the coin very fast 15 times. His hand won't be feeling in the least giddy after that mild exercise so the task of rolling the coin down his nose will be a mere formality. As he acclaims his feat, what he won't have grasped is that the pencilled coin will have left a nice black line right down the middle of his nose.

The Unspiked Drink

Skill Level: ❷
Embarrassment Factor: ❼

Your victim for this prank should be one of those underprivileged souls who are not accustomed to the pleasures of alcohol. You know the sort – the prim spinster of the parish who only ever drinks a single small sherry at social gatherings because "any more makes me feel light-headed" or the quiet little man from the computer department who has half a shandy at Christmas and promptly sticks his tongue down the throat of Mrs Jenkins from kitchenware. Embarrassed by the disgrace (or at least constantly reminded of it by the graffiti on the wall of the gents' lavatory), he will sensibly order nothing stronger than an orange juice at the next leavers' do. But this is where you and your friends tell him that you have spiked his drink with vodka. You haven't really – you've just added a splash of water – but, seduced by the atmosphere and seeing everyone else enjoying themselves, he will soon be convinced that he's been knocking back the spirits. After the first orange juice, he will loosen his tie (the first time that it has been separated from his neck since the Queen's Jubilee) and after the second he will start slurring his speech. By the third, he will be singing and by the fourth he will have taken to the dance floor, swivelling his hips like a latter-day John Travolta. At the end of the evening, even though he won't have touched a drop of alcohol, he will probably have to be carried out horizontally while declaring his undying love for the barmaid. And no matter how many times you tell him the next day that all he was drinking was neat orange juice, he won't believe you. He had a good time – and so did you, watching him.

One Good Turn

Skill Level: ⑩
Embarrassment Factor: ❶

YOU WILL NEED: A PLAYING CARD

This is quite a good wheeze for a party. Hand your victim a pack of playing cards, tell him to go into the next room, to close the door behind him and to turn over, one at a time, as many cards as he wants to. Announce to everyone that when he returns to the room you will immediately name the last card he has turned over. While he is in the adjoining room checking for bugging devices, moving pot plants and hidden cameras, you simply place a card, which you have secretly taken from the pack, on the floor so that it leans upright against the door. As he opens the door to return to the party, he will unwittingly turn over the card and you can claim the easiest of victories.

Fancy That!

Skill Level: ❷
Embarrassment Factor: ❻

Fancy dress parties offer enormous scope for the imagination – the prospect of Margaret Thatcher deep in conversation with Groucho Marx, Napoleon dancing with Catwoman, Fred Flintstone getting off with Marilyn Monroe, and in the kitchen Elvis chatting to Ronald McDonald. They also provide an ideal opportunity for the practical joker, particularly when it comes to sending out the invitations. For just about the most embarrassing thing that can happen to anyone at a party is to be the only one who turns up in fancy dress. So feed your warped sense of humour by telling just one person that it is a fancy dress affair – tell the rest to come in ordinary clothes. However, you need to let them in on the joke in case the victim rings them to compare outfits. Having lit the blue touch paper, you retire and wait for that magical ring of the doorbell when Julius Caesar in all his finery steps into a room full of people in T-shirts and jeans.

Fatal Footwear

Skill Level: ❷
Embarrassment Factor: ❺

YOU WILL NEED:
CARPET TACKS OR DRAWING PINS

None of us would ever dream of looking inside our shoes, trainers or slippers before putting them on because, fortunately, in Britain we don't have to worry about deadly spiders and snakes deciding that our sweaty footwear offers an ideal resting place for the winter. Indeed the biggest threat posed is the emission of noxious fumes from yellowing insoles. The ozone layer has crumbled from less. Taking all of this into account, the toes of footwear make ideal hiding places for all manner of mean tricks, guaranteed to give the wearer a nasty shock. The scattering of a few carpet tacks or drawing pins in the toes of a friend's slippers is assured of waking him up as he staggers out of bed in the morning. Sturdy trainers or shoes also make admirable receptacles for certain semi-liquid substances. Runny rice pudding and creamy porridge are particular favourites, giving that lovely squelchy feel as the toes slide in. Another trick to play on someone who is renowned for his laziness is to tie the laces of his trainers together. If he leaves them tied up every night and simply steps into them the next morning, his first attempt at walking will see him fall flat on his face. This can be strangely rewarding for spectators.

The Reluctant Balloon

Skill Level: ❷
Embarrassment Factor: ❶

YOU WILL NEED:
TWO BALLOONS, STICKY TAPE, A PIN

To the uninitiated, the balloon is a harmless creature, but to nervous souls and Americans a sudden unexpected burst can mean a lifetime in therapy. So this jolly jape can be a good one to play just to see your victim cowering behind the sofa or under the bed waiting for a bang that never comes. To set up the joke, produce an ordinary inflated balloon and ask your victim to stick a pin in it without bursting it. No matter how gently he probes the outer skin, it bursts with an almighty bang, reducing him to a quivering wreck. Tell him he's not trying hard enough – it's easy. Say you'll show him how it's done. Produce a second blown-up balloon but, as you pat it to make sure that it's properly inflated, slip on a piece of transparent sticky tape which was hidden in your hand. Stick the pin through the sticky tape into the balloon and watch as he dives for cover. When nothing happens, he'll feel more than a little foolish, particularly as he emerges to see the big grin on your face.

Blackears

Skill Level: **9**
Embarrassment Factor: **7**

YOU WILL NEED:
INK, A PIECE OF CLOTH

This one is much loved by office workers during those quiet moments when the boss is away, the bar isn't open and there's no racing on the telly. Wait for one of your colleagues to leave the room and, while he is out, smear some ink on the receiver of his phone with a piece of cloth. As he returns to the office, greet him at the door and tell him that there's an urgent call for him on his extension. Depending on his personal circumstances, this could be his wife, lover, bank manager or impotency consultant. Obviously the ink is best concealed on a dark-coloured phone but, with the right incentive, his haste to pick up the receiver should be such that he won't even notice the ink on a pale phone. Of course the first thing he'll realize is that there's nobody on the other end of the line, a situation you explain by saying they must have rung off. But the damage has been done and his ear is now smeared with ink. You can leave him like this for as long as you like, until he looks in the mirror or starts wondering why everyone keeps giving him funny looks.

Room Service

Skill Level: ❸
Embarrassment Factor: ❾

Warning: This trick could be dangerous. Take care!

Spending a couple of nights locked in a hotel on some business course can teach you a few truths about the people you work with, particularly those who steadfastly refuse to buy a round at the bar. They come up with all manner of inventive excuses: "Sorry, I appear to have left my wallet in my room"; "I've just been mugged in the lift"; "What do you mean, you don't accept pesetas in Bridlington?" However you can exact revenge by acquiring a sheet of the hotel's headed notepaper and writing a bogus letter of complaint from the manager to one of your colleagues. The hardest part is actually getting hold of the headed notepaper. Once you've overcome that obstacle, you can get down to the fun part of writing the letter. Something along these lines might be appropriate:

Dear Sir
It is my duty to inform you that I have received a complaint from the hotel chambermaid about the state of room 132 following your stay there on the nights of 18th and 19th February with the group from Wells Electronics. Whilst I appreciate that to an extent what you do in the privacy of your own room is your business, my staff (all of whom are happily married women) were

nevertheless alarmed to discover several items of a sexual nature. Quite apart from the used condoms in the litter bin, there was the matter of the literature in the top drawer of the bedside cabinet. Beneath the copies of What's On in Bridlington and Fun at Filey were two extremely dubious magazines, the covers of which showed leather-clad ladies brandishing whips. The chambermaid was spared further embarrassment by the fact that some of the pages seemed to be stuck together. However, her assistant has been off work since. Finally there was the question of your bed linen. Some of those stains may never come out so I am writing to request that you make a financial contribution of £25 towards a new set of sheets. I look forward to receiving a cheque from you for that amount and suggest that in future you take your trade elsewhere.

Yours faithfully

(Manager)
cc: Mr D. Harding, Managing Director, Wells Electronics

All you have to do now is post the letter near the hotel (to ensure the postmark is authentic) and watch your colleague's anguish as he opens it in the office. Will he be outraged? Will he turn scarlet when he next bumps into his boss? Or will he quietly write out a cheque for £25, explaining that he and his wife have been going through a difficult time and the girl meant nothing to him really?

Thread Bare

Skill Level: ❸
Embarrassment Factor: ❹

YOU WILL NEED:
A COTTON REEL, COTTON THREAD, A NEEDLE

Find a cotton reel with thread the same colour as one of your shirts. Keeping the thread on the reel, push it through the eye of a needle and then push the needle through the sleeve of your shirt. Take away the needle and leave a visible length of thread, something like a couple of inches, hanging on the outside of your shirt. With the reel secreted inside your shirt in such a way that it can be easily unwound, just go about your daily business as usual. Sooner or later, someone will kindly point out that you've got a thread hanging loose and will offer to remove it for you. As they pull, they will unwind the entire thread from the hidden cotton reel. Once someone has started pulling a thread, it's very difficult to stop – there's that natural curiosity to get to the end of it. But as yard upon yard of thread emerges from your shirt, they will be horrified that they've ruined your favourite item of clothing. Any second, they'll be expecting the entire arm to fall apart. No matter when they stop, the feelings of guilt will remain with them until you confess that it's all a joke.

Eggstra ordinary

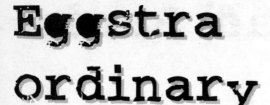

Skill Level: ❸
Embarrassment Factor: ❺

YOU WILL NEED:
AN EGG

If your flatmate is planning to make an omelette for dinner, here's a way of injecting a little entertainment into the proceedings. When you're home alone, hard-boil an egg and replace it in its box. So that your friend is sure to choose the boiled egg, remove any others (you can always claim you fancied a big fry-up earlier). Then cherish the moment as the would-be chef tries in vain to crack the hard-boiled egg on the side of the bowl. There is more chance of the bowl cracking first. As tempers rise, the awful truth will dawn, at which point you can ease the blow by producing an ordinary egg so that nobody need starve. But be warned: you'll probably have to do the cooking for the rest of the week.

The Clingfilm Trap

Skill Level: ❸
Embarrassment Factor: ❾

YOU WILL NEED:
A ROLL OF CLINGFILM

Clingfilm is among the great modern products, yet it is highly doubtful whether its inventors envisaged some of the more unusual – not to say notorious – uses to which it has been put. These include a joke which should only be performed in the home of a very close friend and even then only on condition that you are willing to disinfect the area afterwards. The set-up is simple. Lifting the seat of the toilet, you stretch the clingfilm across the open bowl, making it as smooth as possible to avoid detection. Then you wait for some hapless drunk to stagger to the loo and urinate in the vague direction of the bowl. When you hear a strangulated cry of anguish, you know it's time to get going with the disinfectant.

Mr Lyon

Skill Level: ❸
Embarrassment Factor: ❸

This is really silly and the bane of switchboard operators at almost every zoo, but it never fails to get a laugh in the office. Leave a message on a colleague's phone pad for him to call Mr Lyon and put the number of your nearest zoo or wildlife park. When the long-suffering switchboard operator answers and hears yet another call for Mr Lyon, they will probably politely inform him that he's been the victim of a practical joke. And he will slam down the phone, muttering darkly about having to work with a load of silly kids, while everyone else confirms his views by sniggering like fourth-formers. The more ambitious prankster might try Mr C. Lyon or, for the incurably gullible, Mr L.E. Fant, but don't overdo it so that the joke wears thin. And remember there are dial-back facilities on phones these days so calls can be traced. Your boss wouldn't be too thrilled if the zoo retaliated by depositing two tons of elephant manure outside his office window.

Excalibur

Skill Level: ❸
Embarrassment Factor: ❻

Strange things can happen when you have the builders in – like they actually work for five minutes before taking a tea break – but none stranger than the hand which mysteriously rises out of the sink. You need a certain set of circumstances for this trick to work. The sink must be in place, but without a plughole/drainer or any pipes underneath. There must also be a cupboard under the sink where you can hide. Ideally you could do with the assistance of a third person (maybe one of the builders if he can tear himself away from his Earl Grey) to persuade your partner into taking a closer look at the sink. When she gets near enough, thrust your hand up through the hole in the sink and give her the shock of her life. It is also worth checking in advance that the water is switched off at the mains lest she be tempted to exact immediate revenge.

Hotlips

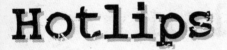 **Skill Level: ❸**
Embarrassment Factor: ❺

YOU WILL NEED:
A BLINDFOLD

Warning: This trick could be dangerous. Take care!

Every party has its self-styled stud, a ridiculously smooth operator over-ripe for sending up. In the Seventies, he wore an open-necked shirt and a medallion, and in the Nineties … he still wears an open-necked shirt and a medallion. He sees himself as the consummate ladies' man and enjoys nothing more than a game where he can come into physical contact with the fairer sex. And naturally he assumes that the feeling must be mutual. So make his dreams come true by telling him that you are going to line up all the girls, blindfold him and ask him to identify each one by the way they kiss. He can hardly contain himself. Once he is blindfolded, though, you have a nasty surprise in store for him, for you quickly substitute men for the girls. As he struts over, lips puckered, to where he thinks the first beauty is awaiting his charms, little does he know that he is about to kiss a 15-stone rugby player. The moment when he realizes to his horror that the person with whom he has just locked lips is not a girl but a burly man is one to dine out on for weeks to come.

Banana Munch

 **Skill Level: ❹**
Embarrassment Factor: ❺

YOU WILL NEED:
A BANANA, A BLINDFOLD

At a party, suggest a game of "Banana Munch", explaining that it involves nothing more complicated than three blindfolded players each racing to devour a banana. Blindfold your victim and give him a banana and then pretend to do the same to the other two participants, but instead merely instruct them to remain silent. On the word "Go", the victim starts to guzzle his banana as rapidly as is humanly possible, convinced that he is part of a race. He will be encouraged in this belief by the shouts of onlookers, all urging him to go faster and telling him that his rivals are catching up. When he has finally swallowed and probably almost choked on the fruit, he triumphantly removes the blindfold, only to be greeted by a sea of grinning faces and the realization that it was a one-horse race.

The Loaded Umbrella

Skill Level: ❸
Embarrassment Factor: ❺

YOU WILL NEED:
CONFETTI OR FLOUR

We come to take certain things for granted: that the supermarket queue we choose will always be the slowest, that Pub comedians will never be funny and that when we open our umbrella nothing will suddenly fall on our head. It is this supreme confidence which makes umbrella-owners a natural target for practical jokers. In their absence, you can slip all manner of objects into a rolled-up umbrella — confetti, flour, paper clips, corn flakes, perhaps even a portion of whitebait — and virtually guarantee that the owner will open the umbrella oblivious to the contents. The first thing he'll know is when a shower of confetti or a shoal of fish comes raining down on his head. The key to obtaining maximum enjoyment from this joke is to make sure you're around when it happens, although the look on his face when you next see him will be a fair indication of whether or not it was successful. Another umbrella trick is to tie up the spokes with tough string, rope or masking tape. When he steps out in the pouring rain and tries to put up his umbrella, he'll find that no matter how hard he tries, it won't open. First he'll get wet and then he'll probably try to get even.

The False Hand

Skill Level: ❹
Embarrassment Factor: ❷

YOU WILL NEED:
A GLOVE, PAPER TISSUES

A lot of adults are just big kids at heart so it is appropriate that some of the best and silliest practical jokes have their origins in the school playground. The much-loved false hand routine definitely falls into that category. The preparation is simple. You fill a glove (including the fingers) with paper tissues so that it looks as if a hand is inside it, then pull down your sleeve over your hand and hold on to the glove by its open end. Do a tour of your friends, offering to shake each one warmly by the hand. As they reciprocate the gesture and shake your hand, it drops off. My, how they'll laugh! Obviously there is a time and a place for such a joke. A high-powered Japanese business delegation might not see the funny side and don't try it out on a little old lady with a dodgy heart. Somehow a joke loses its edge when the victim is rushed to hospital in an ambulance.

The Moving Finger

Skill Level: ❹
Embarrassment Factor: ❸

YOU WILL NEED:
A CARDBOARD BOX WITH A LID, COTTON WOOL, GLUE, TOMATO KETCHUP

This is another joke which owes its conception to the likes of Just William. In those days, it would be guaranteed to send squeamish, pigtailed schoolgirls screaming to the nearest teacher, but in these times of Girl Power you're more likely to receive at least a tongue-lashing or even a severe case of GBH. In the United States, you'd probably be sued for causing unnecessary distress. So this is very much a trick for the brave. Take a small cardboard box and in the bottom cut a hole large enough to accommodate a finger. Glue cotton wool to the bottom of the box, but leave a space over the hole. Close the lid and, holding the box in your hand, push one finger through the hole and bend it over so that it is lying there limply. Tell your victim that you have something interesting to show them, a line which has worked for everyone from Henry VIII to Hugh Grant. Open the box so that they can see the finger and, when they are least expecting it, suddenly wiggle it. You can either have your finger plain or with relish. The addition of tomato ketchup makes the sight of the moving finger all the more horrific and will ensure a spectacular reaction. Once again, there are certain sections of the community on whom it is unwise to practise this trick, notably anyone who has recently lost a finger in a chain-saw accident.

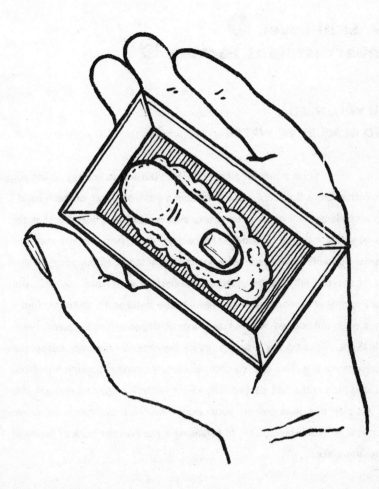

Water Torture

Skill Level: ❹
Embarrassment Factor: ❺

YOU WILL NEED:
TWO GLASSES OF WATER

This is another good prank for a party. Select your victim and say: "I bet you can't recite 'Little Bo Peep' while balancing a glass of water on each hand." Such a challenge will be hard to resist, even when you point out that the glass of water must be placed on the back of each hand. He will still hold his arms out willingly. And as he begins the earnest tale of the poor girl and her lost sheep, a full glass balanced on the back of each hand, you and your friends simply get up and go out. Suddenly the awful truth dawns on him — he has been abandoned without any way of depositing the glasses. He is stuck there, high and dry, although as he becomes increasingly desperate, maybe not so dry. You can, of course, merely pretend to shut the front door and hide in the hall instead. The effect will still be painful enough. It is best to play this joke before your victim has had too much to drink, otherwise he won't be capable of balancing a glass on the back of his hand in the first place.

The Office Mummy

Skill Level: 4
Embarrassment Factor: 6

YOU WILL NEED:
BANDAGES OR MASKING TAPE

It needs at least two people to execute this practical joke successfully. The aim is to catch a work colleague unawares while he is on the phone and tie him to it, using either bandages or masking tape. Since the element of surprise is so important, you need to choose the call carefully. Probably the best time to strike is when he is on the phone to his girlfriend and his thoughts are drifting away aimlessly to a far-off land of romantic candlelit dinners and holidays in the sun. Or of course he may be having a blazing row with her. Either way, his mind will be elsewhere, enabling you and your accomplice(s) to creep up unnoticed. Before he can react, furiously wind the tape or bandage around his head (but not eyes, nose or mouth), the phone and his hand so that he is firmly wedged in position with his ear to the receiver. For good measure, tie his other arm to the arm of the chair. An additional advantage of timing your raid to coincide with a personal call is that his anguished cries down the phone won't alienate a business client. You can leave him like that for as long as you like – you can even spoon-feed him his lunch. Another office jest – one which merely requires the victim to be seated rather than actually on the phone – is to tie him to his chair, using plenty of string or rope. As he sits there helplessly, you can answer all his phone calls with the immortal line: "He's a bit tied up at the moment ..."

Nelson's Eye

Skill Level: ❹
Embarrassment Factor: ❻

YOU WILL NEED:
A CHAIR, A STUFFED STOCKING, A MARBLE, AN OVER-RIPE STRAWBERRY OR PEACH, A BLINDFOLD

This party trick offers a history lesson with a tour of the anatomy of Admiral Nelson. Having been blindfolded, your victim is asked to "feel Nelson's good leg" and her (this one probably works best with a female victim) hands are steered towards someone's leg. Then she is asked to feel Nelson's bad leg whereupon her hands are brought into contact with a chair leg. Next she is asked to feel Nelson's good arm and finds herself fondling an arm before being asked to feel his bad arm, at which she gropes a stuffed stocking. Nothing to get worried about so far, but, in the words of the Caped Crusader, the worst is yet to come. For finally there is the matter of Nelson's eyes. First she must feel Nelson's good eye, whereupon a marble is slipped into her hand, and then it is time for his bad eye. At this moment, her fingers are guided towards a horribly mouldy over-ripe strawberry or peach and as she feels the squashy mess, her screams will be heard in the next hemisphere. One thing is certain – she'll make sure that history doesn't repeat itself.

Something Fishy

Skill Level: ❹
Embarrassment Factor: ❽

YOU WILL NEED:
A PIECE OF UNCOOKED FISH

"Put a haddock in your tank." As an advertising slogan, it stinks. But the result can be more devastating than anything a tiger can produce. It really needs two of you to carry out the plan effectively. First you need to gain access to the engine of the victim's car. This can be done under the pretence of admiring the working parts (for some reason men with new cars are always keen to show off their sumps and carburettors although, as a topic of conversation, it must rank alongside the drainage system of Birmingham or the history of the nail). While your victim is praising his new engine, have your accomplice distract him momentarily – the suggestion (erroneous as it turns out) that there may be a speck of oil beneath the car will guarantee his undivided attention. With his back turned, pull the piece of wet fish from its newspaper wrapping and slip it into the engine near the radiator. When your victim reappears to resume the discussion, bring it to a rapid conclusion by saying that you'd better get back – you've got jobs to do, fish to fry! Now you just let nature take its course. With any luck, the first whiff of fish from the engine will occur while he's on a hot date with a new girlfriend he really wants to impress. On the aphrodisiac scale, the smell of fish comes just above chronic diarrhoea. As a passion-killer, it is comparable to having a policeman knocking on your car window. From then on, the more he drives, the worse the smell will get. Unless you're particularly vindictive, confess your sins before it completely wrecks his love life or before he spends a fortune on garage bills while mechanics search for the fault. As a goodwill gesture, you could always present him with a bag of chips.

Egg On Their Face

Skill Level: ❹
Embarrassment Factor: ❼

YOU WILL NEED:
ONE EGG PER PERSON

One of the most popular games for the dying embers of a party is "Russian Omelette" in which players take it in turns to crack an egg over their own head. All bar one of the eggs are hard-boiled, the excitement being to see which poor partygoer will leave with egg on their face. But if you are a particularly devious host, you can play this game with a minor alteration. The rules are the same – everyone cracks an egg over their head – but to save time and for a grander spectacle, here they will all do it simultaneously. Oh, and there's one other thing which you will omit to mention – none of the eggs have been hard-boiled! Introduce the event by explaining the rules of "Russian Omelette", but don't actually say that is what they are about to play. Merely lead them to believe that all but one of the eggs are safe. On the count of three, get them to smash their eggs on their skull. By the time they realize they've been tricked, it will be too late. With all of your guests sitting there with egg streaming down their faces, it is a handy way of bringing the party to a quick conclusion – but don't be surprised if not everybody comes to your next one.

Spoonerisms

Skill Level: ⑤
Embarrassment Factor: ⑥

YOU WILL NEED:
THREE SPOONS

Warning: This trick could be dangerous. Take care!

You need three people to carry out this practical joke – two accomplices and your stooge. Inform the stooge and one accomplice that they are going to play "Spoonerisms" while the third person acts as umpire. The two participants kneel facing each other, each with a spoon handle in his mouth. They then take it turns to hit the bowed head of their opponent as hard as possible with the spoon. Since it is difficult to exert much force from such a position, the blows should be relatively soft but, unbeknown to the stooge, he is being hit quite firmly by the umpire who has a spoon secreted behind his back. He can be left in ignorance until someone takes pity.

Strung Along

Skill Level: ⑤
Embarrassment Factor: ⑦

YOU WILL NEED:
A LONG PIECE OF STRING

Frighteningly simple, this practical joke relies on your finding two gullible victims in the street. Armed with a length of string, you stop someone who doesn't look in too much of a hurry and, explaining that you are a surveyor whose colleague hasn't turned up, ask him whether he would mind holding one end of the string for a moment while you take the other end for the measurement. You then disappear round a corner with the string and tell the same story to another passer-by, whereupon you vanish into thin air leaving two complete strangers holding a piece of string. If they're still there when darkness falls, you'll know you picked the right men for the job.

The Glass Eye

Skill Level: ❺
Embarrassment Factor: ❺

YOU WILL NEED:
A MARBLE, A HANDKERCHIEF

Hour after hour stuck on the M25 and nothing to do but stare at the bumper of the car in front and listen to Tony Blackburn on the radio. No wonder we have road rage. From time to time, you'll find yourself exchanging sympathetic glances with the driver in the next lane and here's something to do which will really catch his eye. Put a marble in the same pocket as your handkerchief and lift them out together, concealing the marble in the handkerchief. Then, when you're sure you've got his attention, pretend to remove your eye from its socket and to put it on the handkerchief. Keeping the replaced eye tightly shut, produce the marble and polish it furiously with the handkerchief. Your fellow driver will look suitably aghast as you complete the performance by flourishing the marble and appearing to push it back into the socket. When you open your eye, keep the marble hidden in your hand. Even if he realizes that it's a joke, it will relieve the tedium an iota, and if he doesn't, the bumper of the car in front had better watch out.

Public Humiliation

Skill Level: ⑤
Embarrassment Factor: ⑧

Warning: This trick could be dangerous. Take care!

Shopping with your partner can be a tedious experience, so what better way to liven it up than with a spot of public humiliation? Find the most public spot available – in a busy shop or a bank – then suddenly turn to your partner as if you haven't seen him or her for ages (actually this is a joke which is best performed by women on unsuspecting boyfriends or husbands). In an unnaturally loud voice so that nobody within a two-mile radius can fail to hear, say something like: "It's Gerry, isn't it? Fancy seeing you. The last time I saw you, you were just about to start your sex addiction therapy..." Alternative greetings might include:

"You've got a nerve. You go off and screw my mother and now you expect to come crawling back to me and the children."

"Simon, I haven't seen you for years. Did you get off on those bestiality charges? Wouldn't the sheep give evidence?"

Watch with glee as your friend wishes he could crawl in a hole.

Finger Thread

Skill Level: ⑤
Embarrassment Factor: ❷

YOU WILL NEED:
A BANDAGE, A PIECE OF THREAD

This trick is of a gentler nature, but will still work well if you choose a caring, compassionate victim... which immediately excludes lawyers, agents, tax inspectors, traffic wardens, taxi drivers, lorry drivers, bus drivers and anyone carrying a clipboard. To achieve the desired effect, first pierce two small holes in a bandage, placing the holes so that when the bandage is wrapped around your finger they will be on opposite sides of your digit. Then insert a piece of cotton thread through one hole and out the other before wrapping the bandage around your finger. Now all you have to do is go up to that nice lady in the next office and ask her whether she's heard about how you trapped your finger in the filing cabinet. Keeping the bandaged finger behind your back, really lay it on thick about how you had to be rushed to hospital and how the doctors had to sew the tip of your finger back on. At this, produce the bandaged finger for viewing and, sliding the thread up and down so that it looks as if it's going straight through your finger, explain that it doesn't hurt too much if you do it slowly. At the very least, she'll choke on her digestive.

Banana Slice

Skill Level: ❻
Embarrassment Factor: ❹

YOU WILL NEED:
A BANANA, NEEDLE AND COTTON, SCISSORS

Perhaps it has something to do with the shape, but bananas are always the funniest fruit. Any fruit jokes are invariably about bananas, never about apples, oranges or grapes. A banana comedy gig could pack out the Royal Albert Hall whereas a strawberry in concert would struggle to fill a phone box. And when was the last time you had a good laugh with a mango? This prank reinforces the banana's position as the king of fruity comedy. You begin by threading a needle with cotton and pushing it through the skin of the banana along one of the flat sides. Pull plenty of thread through, then push the needle back into the hole and along the next side. Keep going until the needle comes out again through the first hole. Pull both ends of the cotton and the banana will be sliced inside its skin. Repeat this four or five more times, depending on the size of the banana, so that the fruit is sliced from top to bottom. As long as you remember to remove all the threads of cotton, there will be no hint of anything untoward having taken place. Offer your victim the rigged banana and sit back while he peels it… only to find that it is already sliced. One of two things will happen – either the banana will collapse in pieces to the floor or he will simply stare at it in disbelief.

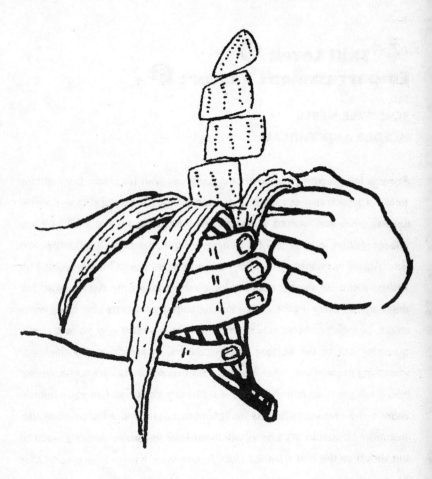

All Sewn Up

Skill Level: ❻
Embarrassment Factor: ❻

YOU WILL NEED:
NEEDLE AND THREAD

Are you fed up with your boyfriend going out with his mates five nights a week? Have you had enough of them commandeering the TV to watch the football while you wanted to see the new Brad Pitt movie? Well here's a way of gaining a degree of revenge without shredding his clothes or chopping off his manhood. It does involve tampering with his wardrobe, but nothing more permanent than sewing up the ends of the sleeves of all his shirts and trousers. In the early morning stupor that passes for being wide awake, he won't notice anything amiss until he wonders why his feet aren't appearing out of the bottom of his trousers. In panic, he may think it's something medical but, when he discovers that his shirts have met a similar fate, it will dawn on him that there is treachery afoot. Tell him you'll unpick them in the evening as long as he agrees to stay in and watch. And in the meantime he could start a new fashion for bank employees wearing T-shirts and shorts to the office...

Conversations With a Pillar Box

Skill Level: 6
Embarrassment Factor: 7

At a loose end for the afternoon? Why not try talking to a pillar-box? Before you know it, you'll have attracted a bigger audience than Channel 5. Your conversation with an inanimate red object operates on the premise that there is an animate pink object inside — namely a small boy who has somehow tumbled in amongst the mail. Of course the trapped toddler is merely a figment of your warped imagination. Choose a post-box on a busy street where there will be plenty of passers-by and start talking through the slot, making reassuring sounds along the lines of "Don't worry, we'll soon have you out of there." Draw the attention of the others to the lad's plight, explaining that you were first attracted by his plaintive cries for help. Say that you've exchanged a few words with him, but that he's now too exhausted to speak. Some uncharitable souls will either think you're a nutter or say it serves the boy right, but there will always be a quorum of good Samaritans willing to lend a helping hand. Before you know it, there'll be half a dozen of you all making soothing noises through the flap. At that point, you calmly melt away into the crowds, your day's work done.

The Tasty Goldfish

Skill Level: ⑥
Embarrassment Factor: ⑤

YOU WILL NEED:
A SLICE OF CARROT, A GOLDFISH BOWL OR FISH TANK

An old favourite, this is nevertheless still a highly effective joke when performed for an unsuspecting public. For maximum effect, it is best carried out in front of a constant stream of passers-by such as in a shop window where it first gained notoriety on "Candid Camera" some 30 years ago. But, failing that, it still works well on a one-to-one basis with a goldfish owner who thinks you've just devoured their pet. The secret of the trick is to conceal a thin, flexible slice of carrot, about three inches long, in the palm of your hand. Dip your hand into the fish bowl or tank and, as you pull it out, produce the piece of carrot and waggle it around as if it were a wriggling goldfish. Before your startled victim can protest, slip it into your mouth and swallow it with a gulp and a licking of your lips. The reaction you get will rarely disappoint.

The Bucket Over Door

Skill Level: 6
Embarrassment Factor: 8

YOU WILL NEED:
A BUCKET OF WATER, A CHAIR

Warning: This trick could be dangerous. Take care!

The bane of every maths teacher since children were invented, the bucket over the door trick remains a classic practical joke. The fact is that nobody expects to open a door and get soaked so the element of surprise makes it a natural winner. Leaving the door slightly open, stand on a chair or step-ladder (you're still trying to trace your real ladder) and balance the bucket of water on the top of the door frame. As soon as the victim pushes open the door, the contents of the bucket will come tumbling down on his head, amid much merriment from all bar one. For the more timid, you could substitute confetti or scraps of paper for water – this has the advantage of not drenching any carpets. At the other end of the scale, there's always baked beans… Just don't use a metal bucket.

Call Box

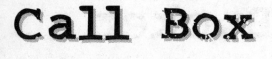

Skill Level: ❼
Embarrassment Factor: ❻

This is another innocuous little pasttime to while away those long hours at the office between lunch and going-home time. For the trick to work, your office window must overlook a public telephone box. The first thing you need to do is pop down to the box and write down the number of the phone there. As you see somebody approaching the box, dial the number so that the phone rings when they open the door. Timing is vital – if you leave it too late, they'll have started dialling their number before you get through and you'll just hear the engaged tone. A smart move is to dial every number except the final one when you first see the person going over to the box and then to press the last digit as they actually enter. Whoever answers the phone will naturally sound puzzled – after all, nobody expects the phone to ring in a call box. Once you've got their attention, you have to give them a task to perform. With any luck, there'll be someone hanging around waiting, maybe for a bus or a lift. Describe that person to them ("fifties, wearing a plastic rain hat, floral coat and wheeling a shopping trolley"), explain that it's your wife, that you knew she'd be outside the supermarket and could they get a message to her? Make it something simple like, "Your husband says, will you get another pork chop for dinner?" At first, the person on the other end is bound to protest, but if you plead convincingly enough, they'll do as you say just to get rid of you so they can use the phone. When you've finally persuaded them, you can watch from the safe haven of your third-floor window as the person in the call box accosts a complete stranger about pork chops. There will be a lot of bemused expressions and arm waving, probably culminating in a suggestion that the poor woman with the shopping trolley comes to speak to you on the phone, in which case you simply hang up. By then, you'll have had your fun. Whilst this may seem a good lark, you have to be sensible about it. Remember that people use call boxes in an emergency so if the person on the other end sounds too harassed, hang up and let them get on with it.

Waterworks

Skill Level: ❼
Embarrassment Factor: ❽

YOU WILL NEED: A BROOMSTICK, A BOWL

Warning: This trick could be dangerous. Take care!

Obtain a goldfish bowl and a broom. Fill the bowl with water (if there is already water in it, remember to remove the goldfish) and promise your victim an astonishing spectacle if he will hold the broomstick while you climb on a chair to reach the ceiling. Carefully place the bowl against the ceiling – open end up, please – and tell the victim to press the broomstick against the base of the bowl, thereby wedging it against the ceiling. Then you climb down from the chair and leave him to get on with it. By the time you return, you'll find either a friend with severely aching arms or a wet carpet.

The Blanket Game

Skill Level: ❻
Embarrassment Factor: ❾

YOU WILL NEED:
A BLANKET

The success of most practical jokes is dependent on the reaction of the victim, so selecting someone with the right credentials for victimization is of considerable importance. "The Blanket Game" will work with anyone, but it is much more satisfying played on somebody meek and mild rather than a natural extrovert. It is best played at a party when everyone has had a few to drink. Even your victim may have downed one or two. He will probably be reluctant to be involved in any game, particularly one where he is the sole participant. After all, he only goes to parties to stand eating sausage rolls in the kitchen where he can trap eaters into conversations about the Bulgarian role in the First World War and the life cycle of the halibut. But you explain patiently that it is nothing more than a guessing game which requires him to sit fully clothed under a blanket. What could be more innocuous? He is told that all the other guests have in mind a certain article which he has about his person and that he must try to guess the article in question by taking it off and displaying it above the blanket.

Only then will he be told if he is right. The odd worry line starts to crease his brow, but it's too late to back out now. This could be the most risqué thing he's done since handing that library book back a day late in 1967. Item by item, he hangs things over the blanket — watch, beige socks, sensible shoes, Postman Pat tie (to make him look wild and reckless) — and item by item, they are rejected. Eventually he finds himself stark naked and utterly confused. The last person to see him naked was the midwife who delivered him, apart from that unfortunate misunderstanding with Mrs Wilkinson at number 22. It is now that everyone joyously confesses that the item they were thinking of was the blanket itself. At this point the blanket may be ceremoniously removed to reveal the poor chap's embarrassment to the full, but a kinder option is to let him keep it on, gather his clothes and scurry to the bathroom… and then probably straight out of the front door.

Water Bed

**Skill Level: ❼
Embarrassment Factor: ❽**

**YOU WILL NEED:
A BOTTLE, A CORK, A PIECE OF STRING, WATER**

For reasons best known to themselves, this trick was apparently once popular with soldiers of the French Army. It works by the theory of frustration. One evening, you slide a bottle full of cold water between the sheets in your victim's bed. Irritated, he will remove it and go to sleep. The following night you do the same, and so, in all probability, will he. On the third night you again insert the bottle of cold water between his sheets, but with a minor adjustment in the form of a piece of string tied from the cork in the bottle to the end of the bed. Angry at discovering the bottle for the third night in a row, he will yank it out of the bed, in the process releasing the cork and a pool of water all over his sheets. It might be an idea to arrange to stay at someone else's house that night...

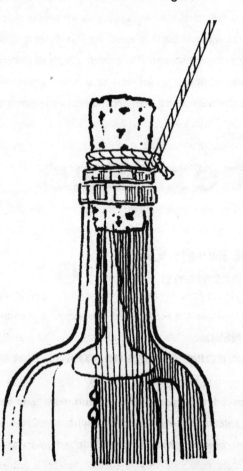

A Fair Cop

Skill Level: 7
Embarrassment Factor: 10

Stag nights are a law unto themselves. Faced with the impending doom of marriage and fortified by copious amounts of lager, the most mild-mannered of men find themselves wandering the streets at night in their underpants, chained to railings or declaring their love to a lamp-post. (It is when they try to consummate the relationship that the police become involved.) But there's another reason why police officers and stag nights are inextricably linked. For one of the most popular features of a stag night is the strippagram. They come in all manner of guises. There's the traffic warden, the nun, the nurse, and the seaside landlady, who'll have you in bed by 10 – and no talking. But for most future grooms, the number one choice is the WPC. Indeed any groom seeing a policewoman arrive at his stag party will immediately assume that she's a strippagram, particularly if he's been told that such entertainment will be provided, and this is a situation which you can use to your advantage and his intense discomfort. What you need to do is pop down to your local police station and have a quiet word in the ear of a friendly officer. Most policemen are enthusiastic about practical jokes as long as there is no real harm done and will cheerfully suggest the services of one of their female colleagues. Persuading her to play along may require a little more of your charm, but a small donation to the Police Benevolent Fund has been known to oil the machinery. When she arrives in uniform at the stag party, the groom will think she's the strippagram and, at the very least, will make a few very non-PC comments. He may even try to get a better look at the stockings and suspenders he is sure she is wearing under her uniform, at which point she will be obliged to produce her ID card and her male colleague. If the groom is still not convinced that he has picked on a genuine officer, the sight of the police car waiting outside should sober him up rapidly.

Jump!

 **Skill Level:** ❽
Embarrassment Factor: ❺

YOU WILL NEED: A STOOL, A BLINDFOLD,. A HARD-BACKED BOOK OR A TRAY

For this trick to be at its most effective, you need a macho man for your victim – someone who reads books about the SAS and keeps pit bull terriers. If your group is composed solely of men who read books about flower arranging and keep toy poodles, try another joke. First you blindfold your victim and perch him on a high stool. Two strong men stand in front of the stool, one at either side, allowing the victim to rest his hands on their shoulders. They then raise the stool off the ground a couple of inches while at the same time another accomplice taps the victim's head firmly with a hard-backed book or a tray. Disorientated by the blindfold, the victim will be certain that the bump was his head hitting the ceiling and that the stool must be high in the air. The two strong men then gently lower the stool to the floor, but the victim's confusion will be such that he'll still think he's several feet off the ground. As everyone urges him to jump, his bravado will almost certainly desert him and he'll decide it's too dangerous. Only when his blindfold is removed will he realize that he's been made to look somewhat foolish.

Apple Pie Bed

Skill Level: ❽
Embarrassment Factor: ❺

After a heavy night, there is nothing more welcoming than your own bed…
that is, unless it is an apple-pie bed. To those ignorant of the genre, an
apple-pie bed is one which it is impossible to penetrate, with the result that
the person, frustrated and exhausted, ends up sleeping on top of the bed
rather than in it. Begin by tucking in the bottom sheet all around the bed
and then add the top sheet, tucking it in at the top and the upper sides. Put
the pillow on top of the top sheet and then fold the top sheet back from
the bottom of the bed so that it covers the pillow. Fold back the top sheet
to reveal the pillow, add blankets and tuck everything firmly in place. From
the outside, the top sheet will look like two sheets, but there is nowhere
for the victim's legs. You have created something which is harder to get into
than Fort Knox.

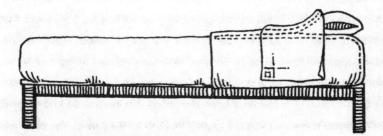

Moving Gnome

Skill Level: ❽
Embarrassment Factor: ❺

Garden gnomes used to be the prerogative of elderly couples living in seaside bungalows with names like "Dunroamin" and "Bayview", but in recent years they have spread alarmingly to other parts of the country and different sections of the community. Nowadays when you walk along any suburban street, you are more than likely to stumble across a gaggle of the bearded chappies peering out from behind a bush or perched on a rock. Clearly they are of limited intelligence – what is the point of holding a fishing rod over a patch of dry soil? – but their simple charm seems to delight their owners. To non-worshippers, the placement of the gnomes may seem haphazard, but we are led to believe that their position in the garden is determined by where they are likely to be happiest – maybe in the sun or near another gnome, or simply a place where next door's tom cat won't spray all over them. So if they were suddenly to start moving around, seemingly of their own accord, it would cause their owners considerable consternation. This is where the practical joker comes in, but remember any such japes should only be carried out on a friend's gnomes. All manoeuvres will have to be performed either in the dead of night or when your friends are out. At first, just move one gnome a couple of feet and wait for any reaction. If, a few days later, the gnome has reverted to its original position, you know that you are getting through to the owner. You can then become bolder in your moves, swapping two of them around. By now the owner will be so perplexed he will probably start confiding in you. And when the next morning he comes down to find Gerald, his favourite gnome, buried head first in the herbaceous border, he will be beside himself. He may even instigate night patrols or erect a barbed-wire fence and searchlights. Meanwhile your deeds become ever more outrageous with gnomes popping up in the strangest places. By the time you have two of them performing an indecent act in the ornamental wheelbarrow, it is probably time to stop.

Press Ganged

Skill Level: ❾
Embarrassment Factor: ❼

Warning: This trick could be dangerous. Take care!

This trick is a real test of your ability to carry out a hoax. Your victim needs to be someone with an unusual hobby. Most offices have them – the little man from accounts who boasts the county's largest collection of pencil sharpeners; or the secretary who goes lawnmower racing at weekends; or the boss who hangs around street corners at night (but that's another story). Collectors, in particular, are always keen for their passion to reach a wider audience. Someone with a room full of toe-nail clippings of the rich and famous can't understand why the rest of the world isn't equally fascinated with the subject, especially as he's hoping to acquire one of Elvis's any day now. Therefore these people are the perfect target for the newspaper hoax. To carry it out effectively, you will need a partner-in-crime, someone with a mobile phone who is willing to pose as a newspaper reporter. Let us say your chosen victim's hobby is collecting toasters. Get your friend to phone him up, pretending to be a reporter with the local paper, saying that he would like to do a story about his collection. Your victim will be only too eager to co-operate, particularly when the "journalist" sounds genuinely interested in toaster collecting. At the end of the first exploratory call, your reporter friend should leave the number of his mobile phone – you don't want the victim phoning up the real paper and finding that no such person exists. The sting will be the photo session. Rather than do this at the victim's house, the paper would much rather take the photos at his workplace where he could be surrounded by appreciative colleagues. The session is fixed for Tuesday and the victim has been asked to bring in as many of his 500 toasters as he can manage. With the aid of his car and two large suitcases, he manages 104. Told that the shoot is to take place in the office at noon, he spends most of the morning hauling toasters upstairs, only to receive a phone call from the bogus reporter at 11.45 telling him that the photographer has been called out on another job. The shoot will be rearranged for Thursday, same time. Not trusting security at work, the victim has little option but to take all his toasters home. He brings them in again on Thursday and again the shoot is cancelled at the last minute as the photographer has suddenly been taken ill. The victim's anger at another cancellation might thus be softened by concern for the photographer's health. Your reporter friend must promise faithfully that he will get a photographer for Monday, adding that the editor is so keen on the story that he would like the avid collector to wear a chef's hat and apron so that it can make a lively front-page picture. Flattery will get you everywhere. Come Monday and the toasters reappear once more. At noon, your victim is standing resplendent in chef's hat and apron, 105 toasters (he managed to cram an extra one in the boot) laid out before him, waiting for the photographer. You have temporarily absented yourself due to an urgent call of nature. You return in one of those disguises so adored by Noel Edmonds, brandishing your daughter's Instamatic. It dawns on your victim that he has been set up. When a toaster flies through the air in your direction, you realize perhaps he can't take a joke after all.

Chapter Two:

Card Tricks

The Hairy Ace

Skill Level: ❶

YOU WILL NEED:
GLUE

Card tricks don't come much easier than this. All you have to do is take a hair (if you're a bit short yourself, borrow one from a friend) and glue it to the back of the ace of hearts so that it is just visible against the background. Since the idea is for the hair to be undetectable to all but yourself, choose a fine strand in preference to a great clump of dreadlock. Select five cards from the pack (including the hairy ace) and ask your friends to lay them face down on the table. By the magical powers invested in you, tell them that you can find the ace of hearts without even touching any of the cards. Although you can spot the ace straight away by the presence of the hair, make a great play of locating the correct card – you don't want everyone to know how easy it is. After your first success, have the five cards rearranged and repeat the feat. You can carry on ad infinitum, the only threat to success being if one of your houseproud friends decides to "get rid of that nasty little hair on the back of one of the cards."

Royal Family

 **Skill Level:** ❶

Put all 12 court cards (jacks, queens and kings) together somewhere in the centre of the pack and ask a member of your audience to try and split them up by cutting the cards a dozen times. With each cut, take at least three cards off the pack. Even after the 12 cuts, the entire royal family will, barring divorce or skiing holidays, still be together in the pack.

Odd One Out

Skill Level: ❶

YOU WILL NEED:
A PAPER CLIP

This is extremely silly, but can lead to immense frustration. Indeed people have been known to come to blows over it. All you do is pluck five cards from the pack – two pairs and an odd one. For example, you might choose the two of spades, two of diamonds, 10 of hearts, 10 of diamonds and queen of spades. Hold all five cards together in your hand with the odd card in the middle of the five. Show the faces of the cards to your volunteer and then reverse them so that he is confronted with the backs of the five cards.

Tell him you're going to ask him to do the easiest thing in the world, a task which is even within the intellectual capabilities of the average amoeba: would he kindly attach a paper clip to the odd card? With confidence oozing from his pores, he slides the clip on to the middle card but, when you reverse the cards once more to show them face up, it transpires that he has put the paper clip on the front card by mistake. He's bound to demand another go… and another… and another, and as he continues to meet with abject failure, that's when matters can become a little heated. What make it all the more galling is that you are clearly not interfering with the cards or the clip in any way. It's just one of those irritating little tricks.

Secret Signals

Skill Level: ❶

YOU WILL NEED:
A TABLE

By squatting under a perfectly ordinary table, with no view of proceedings, you are somehow able to name the cards which are being dealt on top of it. The secret of the trick is that one of the dealers is your partner-in-crime and the pair of you have concocted a series of signals which he will relay to you under the table with his right hand. If the card is a spade, he will tap once on his right knee; if it is a club, he will tap twice; for a heart, he will tap three times; and for a diamond, four times. After he has indicated the suit, he will move on to the actual number with the jack counting 11, the queen 12 and the king 13. Thus two taps followed by a display of 12 fingers tells you that the card which has been dealt is the queen of clubs. If your accomplice is subtle with his signals, the rest of your friends will be baffled by your prowess. Their initial suspicions will fall on the cards, so make sure they shuffle them to their satisfaction before dealing, and on the table. Perhaps there is a hole in it. So allow them to carry out a thorough inspection of the table for woodworm or any other boring parasite. They will find nothing untoward and will be left with little option but to acknowledge your brilliance… until someone starts wondering why your accomplice suddenly seems to have such an itchy right knee.

Sneak Preview

Skill Level: ❷

Ask someone to pick any card from the deck and then tell them to show it to the rest of the gathering, but not yourself. While all eyes are focused on that card, take a sneaky glance at the bottom card in the deck… and whatever you do, don't forget it. Ask your volunteer to put the selected card back on top of the deck face downwards and then, as you deliver your well-honed patter, casually cut the pack anywhere you like. Square off the deck so that there can be no suspicion of an improper cut, fan through the cards and the selected card will be immediately beneath the one you glanced at earlier. It's as easy as that.

Bottoms Up

Skill Level: ❷

Even if the only deck of cards you're familiar with is the old Max Bygraves classic (15 weeks in the charts in 1973), you should be able to master this simple trick. Before you begin, secretly turn the bottom card of the pack face upward. Then fan out the cards in your hand face down, making sure you don't show the rogue end card, and invite your guinea pig (metaphorical, not literal) to pick a card. At this point, it is a neat diversion to proffer a particular card whereupon your guinea pig, smelling a rat, will think that the trick revolves around a hidden card and will deliberately select another. This will make the eventual dénouement all the more stunning. When the person has chosen a card, close the pack and swap it into your other hand, in the process turning the pack over so that the odd card is now face down on top. After asking the person to remember the selected card, get him or her to return it to the pack. Turn your back on proceedings, fan open the cards and you can easily identify the chosen card as it will be the only one, apart from the top card, which is face down. With the sure-fire scent of victory in your nostrils, turn around and demand: "Is this your card?" When the gasps of amazement have subsided, savour the moment as your friends applaud wildly and, with any luck, start writing cheques.

Talking Cards

Skill Level: 2

YOU WILL NEED:
12 IDENTICAL ENVELOPES, A PENCIL

Your friends may long have suspected that there was something strange about you – perhaps it's your back collection of "Songs of Praise" videos or your bedroom poster of Judith Chalmers. Now you can confirm their worst fears as you claim that playing cards are able to talk to you. Before carrying out this trick, you need to lay your hands on a dozen identical envelopes. Mark four with a tiny pencil dot on the left-hand corner of the flap, four with a dot on the right-hand corner of the flap and leave the remainder blank. Then put the envelopes in a pile, the left-dotted on top, the right-dotted in the middle and the blank underneath. With the preparation complete, it's time for the magic. Remove the four jacks, the four queens and the four kings from the pack and put a jack in each of the top four envelopes (those with the dot on the left), a queen in the next four (those with the dot on the right) and a king in the last four blank ones. Turn the envelopes over so that nobody can see the dots and get someone to give them a good shuffle. It is now that, picking up one envelope at a time, you claim to hear voices from within. If the dot is on the left, you could claim the voice is "Jack Nicholson or maybe Jack (sic) Villeneuve, but whoever it is, it's definitely a jack." You then open the envelope to reveal the jack and prove your amazing psychic powers. Continue through as many of the remaining envelopes as your audience can stomach and wait for the men in white coats to take you away.

Telephone Telepathy

Skill Level: ❷

With this trick, you can achieve the seemingly impossible by transferring your thoughts of a particular card down the phone so that the person at the other end names it correctly. Shuffle the pack thoroughly and allow your audience to inspect it in order to verify that the cards are perfectly ordinary and are not marked in any way. Thus assured, they will find what follows all the more remarkable. Ask one person to select absolutely any card from the pack and to show it to you. Let's say it's the six of diamonds. Then you boldly declare that you will telephone your friend Vic and, without you giving him any clues whatsoever, he will tune in to your telepathic powers and identify the card. Needless to say, it's all a big con. When you ring up, Vic, who has been thoroughly briefed, answers the phone and, speaking slowly, says: "Clubs, diamonds, hearts, spades." When he reaches the correct suit (here it would be diamonds), you speak, saying something like: "Is Vic there?" (Cue song). He then counts through the numbers, slowly and deliberately, starting from the ace and working up to the king. When he gets to the correct number (in this case the six), you speak again, saying: "Hi, Vic, I've got a call for you." You then pass the phone to whoever chose the card in the first place and Vic promptly declares that the card is the six of diamonds. Impressive, eh?

Kings and Queens

Skill Level: ❸

This trick comes complete with its own fairytale – the story of a group of travelling kings and queens who are forced to swap coaches because of insufficient leg room. Begin by removing all of the kings and queens from the pack and arrange the eight cards in suits so that they alternate king, queen, king, queen. Deal out the first pair – the king and queen of hearts – face down and ask someone to turn them over. While this is happening, craftily switch the top card of the six remaining in your hand to the bottom, thereby changing the order of the royal rulers. With the king and queen of hearts still face up, deal out the other six cards alternately face down so that the audience, unaware of your sleight of hand, will think that all the kings are in one group and all the queens are in the other. Then you can tell your tale of how the various royals set off to a ball in two separate coaches, divided by sex. After a while, the king of hearts, who, although married to the queen of hearts, was having an affair with the queen of diamonds and also had a secret love child by the six of spades, felt that travelling with three men was cramping his style and his legs, so he decided to switch to the queens' coach. At this point you move the king of hearts face up to the other pile which supposedly contains four queens. However, the queen of hearts didn't want to share a coach with her errant husband. She knew all about his flings and anyway she was about to "come out" about her relationship with the queen of clubs, so she decided to move over to the kings' coach. At this point, you move the queen of hearts (face up) to the other pile, that which is thought to contain three kings. Thus you have one pile with the king of hearts face up and three cards face down and the other pile with the queen of hearts face up and three cards face down. Everyone thinks the queen of hearts is with three kings and the king of hearts with three queens. But, as with most royal romances, nothing is quite what it seems and you turn over the cards to reveal that, in fact, all the kings are in one coach and all the queens are in the other.

Bermuda Triangle

 **Skill Level:** ❸

YOU WILL NEED: A PRITT STICK

With this trick, you demonstrate how a perfectly ordinary card can vanish completely from the pack. The trick is in the preparation. While your fans are still paying at the turnstiles, smear the four edges of the back of the top card with a Pritt stick (and maybe a blob in the middle for luck). When everyone is seated and a hush has descended on the auditorium (all right, your bed-sit), ask a volunteer to take a card, to show it to the rest of the audience and to put it on top of the pack. Under no circumstances must your volunteer be allowed to take the original top card. As you pick up the pack, casually press the chosen top card down on to the sticky back of the card beneath. They will now be as one. Cut the pack a few times and deal out the cards face up. Handling the two glued together cards carefully, express concern that there is absolutely no sign of the selected card – it has simply vanished into thin air. At this point, some over-zealous members of your audience may demand a body search lest the missing card be secreted about your person. This should be actively encouraged unless the audience is:

a)   composed entirely of serial killers on a care in the community day-release scheme

b)   a Women's Institute party

c)   the Dale Winton Appreciation Society

Mistaken Identity

Skill Level: ❸

Take the four aces from the pack and, when nobody is looking, slip the ace of diamonds into your pocket. Hold up the other three aces in a fan shape with the ace of hearts in the middle but so that its true identity is hidden by the ace on either side. As far as the audience are concerned, it is the ace of diamonds in the middle. Boldly announce that you are going to make the ace of diamonds disappear. Gather up the three aces, put them in different parts of the pack, give them a good shuffle and deal them out face up. To everyone's surprise, there is no sign of the ace of diamonds. Complete the illusion by producing the ace of diamonds from your pocket.

Rhyming Cards

🦉 **Skill Level:** ❸

All you need to do for this trick is memorize the following rhyme:

"Eight kings threaten to save

95 queens for one sick knave."

It is utterly meaningless until you translate it into cards – eight, king, three, 10, two, seven, nine, five, queen, four, ace, six, jack. So, before attempting this feat of memory, arrange the cards in the pack in that order and in alphabetical suit order of clubs, diamonds, hearts and spades. Thus the first card will be the eight of clubs, followed by the king of diamonds, then the three of hearts, 10 of spades, two of clubs, seven of diamonds, nine of hearts and so on. In this way, you can predict the order of every card in the pack. Your suspicious friends can inspect the cards to their hearts' desire, but will find nothing to explain your powers. For the cards are not marked in any way and, to the untrained eye, appear stacked totally at random. The experience will leave them completely mystified… and asking for your help with next week's Lottery numbers.

Spot the Dot

Skill Level: ❸

YOU WILL NEED:
A PENCIL

To prepare for this trick, use a soft pencil to draw a diagonal line across the side of the shuffled deck of cards. Your audience will attribute the pencil line to everyday wear and tear, little suspecting that it is all part of your fiendish plan. For the trick itself, ask one person to pick a card and, without showing it to you, to memorize it and replace it anywhere in the deck. The chosen card will now show up as a small dot in the side of the deck and is thus easily identifiable, allowing you to brandish the card triumphantly to your new-found fan club

In a Flap

Skill Level: ❸

YOU WILL NEED:
TWO EXTRA CARDS, SCISSORS, GLUE

Cut a small square from the middle of one spare card, fold it in half and stick one half to the back of the other extra card. This gives that card a small flap. Press down the flap so that it is invisible (for this reason the cards must have identical patterns on the back) and put it on the top of the pack. Now announce that you are going to suspend the cards in mid-air. Place the top card face up in the palm of your hand, secretly pull out the flap and grip it between your fingers. Put a number of other cards on your hand, cunningly inserting them beneath the card with the flap. Then when you turn your hand over, instead of falling to the floor, the cards will be held in place by the trick card. You don't get tricks like this with David Copperfield...

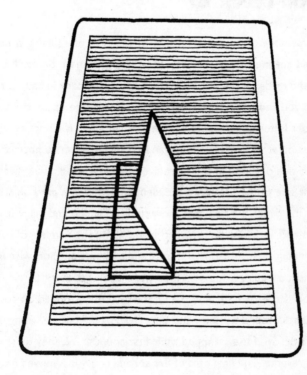

Q Card

 **Skill Level: ❸**

Entrust a member of your audience with the task of shuffling a pack of cards. Avoid anyone of a particularly nervous disposition, or you'll end up picking all the cards off the floor. Tell them to cut the pack in half, to return one half to you and to arrange the remaining cards face up on the table in the shape of a letter Q, complete with tail. When the Q is complete, silently count the number of cards in the tail and count the same number of cards up the right side of the Q. If there are five cards in the tail, count five cards up the right side of the Q. Write the identity of that fifth card on a slip of paper, fold the paper over so that the writing is hidden and place it in the centre of the Q. Ask your assistant to count aloud the number of cards in the Q, beginning at the bottom of the tail and then moving clockwise up the left-hand side, stopping wherever they wish. Then get them to count the same number backwards around the Q, the card they stopped on counting as 1, going back around the left-hand side, avoiding the tail, and going up the right-hand side. So if they stopped their first count at 12, they must count 12 cards in reverse. The final card of this second count is removed from the Q and the piece of paper opened. If everyone has done their sums properly, the paper should bear the name of the final card.

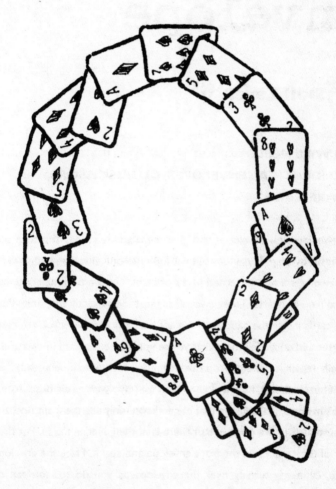

The Double Envelope

Skill Level: ❸

YOU WILL NEED:
TWO IDENTICAL ENVELOPES, GLUE, SCISSORS,
A SPARE CARD

Take two identical envelopes and glue them address sides together so that there is no overlap. The end result will look like one envelope with two backs. From two identically patterned packs of cards, choose two matching cards – say, the nine of hearts. These two cards must look exactly the same. Put one of the cards inside the back envelope and seal it down. Now you are ready to face your audience. Tell them that you're going to cut a card in two and then magically repair it. Take the top card from the deck (you have already put the nine of hearts there), hold it aloft and cut it in two with a pair of scissors. Pick up the envelope, making sure that the audience only see the front one, and tip it up so that they are positive that there is nothing hidden inside. Put the two halves of the card inside the front envelope and seal it. Place the envelope on a table, cunningly turning over the envelope as you do so. You can count yourself extremely unlucky if anyone spots your deception. Now the back envelope is face up. Expressing trepidation as to the outcome, unseal the flap of the back envelope and pull out the card – a magically repaired nine of hearts.

Pocket Calculator

Skill Level: ❹

Before facing your audience, slip two cards into your pocket. For the purposes of this trick, it might be an idea to wear a jacket since the sight of men rummaging around in their trouser pockets can be unnerving. Added to which, there's always the danger that the cards could get stuck to a 1979 blackcurrant Spangle. Get someone to shuffle the pack and, after this has been done to mutual satisfaction, deal the top three cards face up. Ask your volunteer to concentrate on any one of the three cards. Meanwhile make a mental note of the three cards and in which order they occur. Put them in that order in your jacket pocket behind the other two cards already there and announce that you will predict which card the volunteer has chosen. Take the two cards from the front of your pocket (the ones hidden there before the trick) and replace them in the pack. Ask the person, who now thinks there's only one card in your pocket, to name the card which he or she has been thinking of. As long as you have correctly remembered the order of the three cards left in your pocket, you should have no trouble in producing the right one.

Double Dealing

Skill Level: ❹

Here you can astound your friends by changing one card into another without any visible chicanery. Ask someone to choose a card, to show it the rest of the gathering without letting you see it, to remember it and put it back on top of the deck. Create some diversion so that nobody looks at your hands (a fire alarm is probably excessive), hold the pack in your left hand and use the index finger and thumb of your right hand to bend the top two cards upwards, lifting them off as one. Show the audience what they think is the top card (in reality it is of course the second card) and study the look of bewilderment on their faces. Put the two cards back on top of the pack, give the deck a magic tap and this time turn over the top card only... and it will be the chosen card. Given the innate simplicity of this trick, it is best to perform it either to an audience of dullards or to people who are all too drunk to care.

Lookalikes

Skill Level: ❹

For this trick you need two sets of pairs which look similar – such as the seven of clubs and seven of spades and two of diamonds and two of hearts. Remove all four cards from the pack. Place the seven of clubs on top of the pack and the two of diamonds at the bottom. Keep the other two face down to one side. Announce that without any physical interference or mental coercion, you will predict the precise place in the deck at which your volunteer tells you to stop dealing and that you will mark the spot in advance with two lookalike cards. Sounds impossible, doesn't it? Read on. Deal the cards face down, telling your associate to say "Stop" whenever he or she wishes. When the call comes, pick up the two of hearts and lay it face up on top of the dealt cards. Place the rest of the pack on top of the two of hearts. Deal from the top of the pack again and this time when the call to stop arrives, put the seven of spades face up on top of the dealt cards. As before, put the rest of the pack on top of the seven of spades. Cut the cards at the upturned two of hearts and reveal the card immediately above it – the two of diamonds. Then do the same with the seven of spades, the card above it being the seven of clubs. Eat your heart out, Mystic Meg.

Partners

Skill Level: ❹

Magician's assistants are a breed apart. Where else would you find a woman prepared to smile sweetly whilst being sawn in half? For this trick, your assistant is indeed your most valuable prop as you hang on her every word to bemuse, baffle and bewilder the audience. It all revolves around a secret code concocted beforehand between the two of you. The trick begins with you leaving the room. In your absence, someone picks a card and your assistant shows it to all present before carefully placing it face down on the table. The card is not marked in any way, but the first clue from your assistant is in the direction the card is facing. Beforehand the pair of you have agreed that the suit shall be determined by the table representing an imaginary clock. If, from the door, the card is pointing on a 12 o'clock/6 o'clock axis, it means the card is a spade; a 9 o'clock/3 o'clock axis denotes a club; 2 o'clock/8 o'clock indicates a heart; and 10 o'clock/4 o'clock suggests a diamond. So the moment you enter the room you know what suit the card is. Now watch your assistant's movements very closely. If she flicks imaginary dust from her knee, your pre-arranged code will tell you the card is an ace, a two or a three; if she touches her hair with her right hand, it's a four, five or six; if she touches her hair with her left hand, it's a seven, eight or nine; if she casually crosses her arms, it's the 10, jack, queen or king; if she starts fidgeting on the spot, she's probably waiting to go to the loo. To identify the precise card, you need to indulge in a spot of carefully rehearsed conversation with your assistant, but try and make it sound as natural as possible instead of like a school nativity play. Each of your assistant's replies carries a hidden meaning. When you ask cautiously, "Is the card a club?" or whichever suit you know it to be, if she answers "Yes", it is the first card in the group indicated by her movements. If she answers "It is", then it's the second card in the group. If she replies "Right", it's the third in the group. And if she answers "Correct", it's the fourth in the group. Therefore if you enter the room, see the card on the table on a 9 o'clock/3 o'clock axis, see your assistant touching her hair with her left hand and when you ask her whether the card is a club she replies "It is", then you can immediately declare the mystery card to be the eight of clubs. This is not a trick to repeat too often in front of the same people as it's only a matter of time before someone cracks your code.

7 Up

Skill Level: ❹

Arrange the cards in advance so that the seven of hearts is reversed and placed seventh from bottom of the pack. Fan the pack, making sure that nobody can see the reversed card, and ask someone to choose any card, to remember it and to return it to the top of the deck. Cut the cards so that the reversed seven is now somewhere near the middle. Explain in hushed tones that one of the cards has somehow managed to turn itself over and that the value of that card will pinpoint the precise whereabouts of the selected card. Search through the pack until you find the upturned seven of hearts, count along another seven cards and, lo and behold, the seventh card will be the chosen one.

The Tapered Deck

 **Skill Level:** ❹

YOU WILL NEED:
A PAIR OF SCISSORS

This trick is best performed with a fairly old pack since the first thing you have to do is cut strips off all the cards. To produce what is known in the trade as a tapered deck, you have to make narrow sloping cuts down either side of every card so that one end of each card is slightly narrower than the other. This can be a time-consuming business, so if you have a low boredom threshold, move on to the next trick in the book. Making sure that all the cards are facing the same way (ordinary edge outwards), fan them out and offer them to a member of your audience. Ask him or her to pick a card and study it in total silence. Make sure they are fully aware that any attempt to speak will result in a severe punishment. While this thought process is taking place, put the cards back together, turn them around and fan them out again, this time with the narrow edge facing outwards. Tell the person to put the card back anywhere in the pack. Put the cards behind your back and regroup them into a neat pile. Say that you will only be able to find their card if they concentrate really hard on it whereas in truth all you have to do is feel out the card which is wider than the others at one end.

Grains of Truth

Skill Level: ④

This is another crafty way of recognizing a chosen card. Ask a volunteer (preferably someone who is not in possession of all their faculties) to shuffle the pack and to separate the cards into two piles. Tell him or her to choose any card from the first pile, study it and put it back on top of the second pile. As you do so, tap the top card on the second pile to indicate where you want them to put it, in the process cunningly releasing a few grains of salt you had concealed between your thumb and forefinger. Unless they are particularly alert, they will not spot the ruse. Then ask them to place the first pile on top of the second pile and to turn the whole pack face up. Tap the side of the pack with your finger (or a magic wand if you are treating all this seriously), warble some magic incantation, and the presence of the salt, allied to the tapping, will create a small gap immediately above the chosen card. You simply pull out the card beneath the space and take a bow.

Suit ability

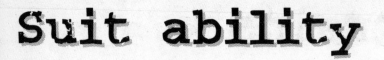 **Skill Level:** ❹

Beforehand, sort the pack into two halves, one containing spades and hearts, the other clubs and diamonds. Put the two halves together, but make sure that the top card of the bottom half protrudes slightly in order to act as a marker. Your friends will think this is a perfectly ordinary pack of cards – a random mix of red and black – but you know different. Now to baffle them. Using the marker card as your dividing line, separate the pack into your two carefully prepared halves. Ask someone to pick any card from one half of the pack, to show it to everyone else in the room except yourself and then to replace it anywhere in the other half of the pack. All you have to do is flick through the cards and spot which spade or heart has managed to infiltrate its way into the half reserved for clubs and diamonds, or vice-versa. To sustained applause (and maybe a few encores), hold the chosen card aloft.

Odds'n'Evens

Skill Level: 4

Remove the court cards from the pack and put all the odd numbers (aces, threes, fives, sevens and nines) in one half and all the even numbers (twos, fours, sixes, eights and 10s) in the other half. Fanning out one half of the reduced pack face down, ask someone to select a card and study it. While this is happening, quickly square up that half and fan out the second half instead. Ask for the card to be replaced anywhere in those cards. By looking through the cards, you can easily spot the chosen one – it will be the only even-numbered card amongst the odds, or vice versa.

Telepathy

 **Skill Level:** ❹

YOU WILL NEED: A BLINDFOLD

The actual degree of skill required to perform this trick is minimal – there is no sleight of hand – but as a memory test it takes some beating. For a successful result, you and your trusty assistant need to burn the midnight oil to think of a code which will enable you to identify any card in the pack – something along these lines:

ACE	=	TELL ME
TWO	=	CAN YOU TELL ME?
THREE	=	WILL YOU TELL ME?
FOUR	=	PLEASE TELL ME
FIVE	=	ARE YOU ABLE TO TELL ME?
SIX	=	NAME
SEVEN	=	CAN YOU NAME?
EIGHT	=	WILL YOU NAME?
NINE	=	PLEASE NAME
10	=	ARE YOU ABLE TO NAME?
JACK	=	CONCENTRATE AND TELL ME
QUEEN	=	PLEASE CONCENTRATE AND TELL ME
KING	=	CONCENTRATE AND TRY TO NAME

CLUBS	**=**	**THE CHOSEN CARD**
DIAMONDS	**=**	**THIS PERSON'S CARD**
HEARTS	**=**	**THE MYSTERY CARD**
SPADES	**=**	**THE CARD WHICH HAS BEEN SELECTED**

After committing that lot to memory, all you have to do is astound your audience by your telepathic powers. While you are blindfolded, your assistant asks someone to pick any card from the pack, shows it to the rest of the audience and then asks you to name it. And it is the way in which your assistant phrases the question that gives you the card's identity. For example, if the assistant says, "Please name the mystery card", your memory should tell you that it's the nine of hearts. It doesn't always to pay to come up with the right answer too quickly – otherwise everyone will know it's a fix – so grope around in the dark for a while with comments like: "I see a red card... I see eight dots... no, no, I see nine...", or "I see a tall dark handsome stranger... it's the king of clubs."

The Marked Pack

 **Skill Level:** ❹

YOU WILL NEED:
A PENCIL, A SMALL BOX

The essence of a good card trick is for it to appear fiendishly difficult to perfect yet in practice be incredibly easy. With this trick, all of the hard work is done beforehand. Firstly, remove any card from the pack (let's say it's the king of hearts) and on the back of the card make a small pencil mark so that you will be able to identify it when the need arises. Then along the bottom border of the face of every other card write "king of hearts". Once you've recovered from writers' cramp, shuffle the cards and fan them out face down to your volunteer, making sure that the writing is hidden from view. While you are spreading the cards, you are mentally searching for the card with the pencil mark on the back. When you find it, casually remove it from the pack as if you have just plucked any card at random. Pretend to write on its face (but don't) and then put the card in the box without letting your volunteer see which card it is. Ask him to select any other card from the pack, but again make sure he doesn't see its face. Since they've all got "king of hearts" written on them, it doesn't matter which card he picks. Drop the card into the box and move the rest of the cards out of the way. Now for the revelation. Take the two cards from the box and show the card supposedly chosen by you (in reality, of course, it's his). Across the bottom is written "king of hearts" and, when the second card is turned over, amazingly it is indeed the king of hearts. In the words of David Coleman: "Quite remarkable."

Piles

Skill Level: ❹

In spite of its name, this trick is extremely popular at parties. Rig the pack in advance by putting six picture cards at the top and the other six at the bottom. Then ask the audience to call out any four cards with values between one and 10 (i.e., not picture cards) and remove them from the pack to leave a deck of 48. Deal these cards into six piles of eight so that, unbeknown to the audience, the top and bottom card of each pile will be a picture card. Choose someone from the audience to take a card from near the centre of any of the six piles, to show it around (but obviously not to you) and to put it back on top of the same pile. Tell them they can stack the piles in any order. Announce that by looking through the pack, you will immediately be able to spot the mystery card. Since the chosen card was from the centre of a pile it will not be a picture card but, when replaced on top of a pile and stacked with the other piles, it will finish up between two picture cards. So all you have to do is flick through the pack and find the only non-picture card between two picture cards. The sole exception is if the person has arranged the pile with the chosen card at the top of the pack, in which case the top card will not be the picture card you are expecting, but the mystery card itself.

Blind Sums

Skill Level: ⑤

Discard the twos, threes, fours, fives, sixes and jokers from the pack to leave 32 cards. Explain that this trick operates under a points system whereby an ace counts as 11, a court card (jack, queen, king) as 10 and all the others as numbered. Turn your back on proceedings and ask three people to choose one card each from the reduced pack and to put them separately face up on the table. Then tell them to add the number of cards needed to bring each pile's points total up to 15. So if the upturned card is an ace, four cards should be placed face down on the same pile; if it's a king, five cards should be added face down; if it's an eight, seven cards should be added. They must then hand the remaining cards to you. Since your back has been turned throughout, you can have no idea which three cards were originally selected, but boldly declare that by counting the number of cards you have just been given and adding 16 you will arrive at the total points score of the three upturned cards. It never fails.

Queens Behaving Badly

 **Skill Level:** ⑤

Line up this trick by removing the four queens and two jacks from the pack. Fan out the queens in your left hand so that everyone can see them... but not the two jacks which are hidden behind the second queen. As far as everyone can see, you are only holding four cards. Gather up the cards and place them on top of the pack. Then spin some yarn about the househusband kings complaining about being left at home with the ironing while the queens are out enjoying themselves at a hen night down at the local. Say that, on the kings' orders, you're going to split the women up by putting one queen on the bottom of the pack, two well apart in the middle and the fourth one on top. Take the top card and put it on the bottom of the pack, making sure that all present can see that it is a queen. Take the next two cards and place them well apart in the centre of the pack, but keep their identities hidden as these are the two jacks. Show everyone the fourth card – a queen – and replace it on top of the pack. Ask a volunteer to cut the pack, but confess that, despite your best efforts, the four queens have somehow managed to gang up together again. Deal out the pack of cards face up and, somewhere around the middle, all four queens will be together.

Jumping
Jacks

Skill Level: ⑤

To set up this variation on "Queens Behaving Badly", take the four jacks from the pack along with any three other cards. Show the four jacks to your audience in a fan with the three rogue cards hidden behind the third jack. Square the cards up and put them on top of the pack before dealing the first four cards (which the audience foolishly believe to be the quartet of jacks) into separate rows. Now deal the next three cards (which really are three jacks) on top of the first jack. Continue dealing out three cards on to each of the other rows so that you have four piles of four. The audience will think there is a jack at the bottom of each pile, but you know that the pile on the left consists solely of jacks while the remaining three piles are made up of random cards. Pick up the first pile and confirm the audience's misconception by showing them the jack at the bottom. Stack this pile on top of the next one, put these two piles on top of the third and then the three piles on top of the fourth. Make sure you don't let anyone see the bottom card of the last three piles. With all 52 cards together, get members of the audience to cut the pack as many times as they wish. Reveal that the jacks which, moments ago, were at the bottom of separate stacks are now magically reunited. And sure enough when you fan out the cards face up, all four jacks are together.

Sliced Open

Skill Level: 5

YOU WILL NEED:
A KNIFE

Ask someone to pick a card and to show it to the rest of the audience. While this is happening, and Great Aunt Edie who has forgotten her glasses and thinks she's looking through old family photographs is consequently regaling all around her with tales of how she knew the queen of clubs when she was just a girl, you should secretly squeeze the cards so that they buckle a little. Then ask for the card to be put back on the bottom of the pile. Shuffle the cards repeatedly until everyone is satisfied that the cards are well and truly mixed up. Because all of the cards apart from the chosen one have been buckled, there will always be a discernible break, no matter how thoroughly they are shuffled. Pick up a knife and slide it into the pack at the point of the break. The card below the break should be the one chosen earlier. The amount of buckling required to perform this trick successfully comes only with practice. Obviously the less you need to bend the cards the better, as it won't be apparent to the audience what you are up to. If you bend them at right angles, it does tend to give the game away.

The Three Pack Trick

 **Skill Level:** ⑤

YOU WILL NEED:
A PENCIL

To get ready for this trick, choose any card from the pack and mark it lightly on the back with pencil dots in the top-left and bottom-right corners. Replace it in the pack so that it is the 26th card from the top. Now for the trick. Place the pack face down on the table. This is pile A. Ask a volunteer to lift off more than half the cards and to place them on the right to form pile B. It is essential that over half of the cards are lifted otherwise the trick won't work and you'll be left looking a complete dipstick. Now ask your associate to lift off about half of the cards on pile B and to put these on the right to form a third pile, unsurprisingly known as pile C. Next ask him or her to shuffle pile C, to look at the top card, memorize it and put it back on top of that pile. Then order pile C to be placed on top of pile B and ask for pile A to be shuffled and put on top of the B and C pile. Finally pick up the cards and spread them out face down from left to right. When you see the pencil dot on the marked card, count it silently as 1 and continue counting the cards to yourself until you reach 26. If you get to the end of the row before reaching number 26, go back to the left-hand end and carry on counting. Turn over the 26th card and, joy of joys, it will be your friend's chosen card.

Mind Reading

 **Skill Level:** ⑤

In common with a number of tricks, this one relies on you snatching a quick glance at the bottom card in the pack when nobody is looking. The premise may be straightforward, but the result is highly impressive as you demonstrate powers of mind-reading which would put "The Champions" to shame. You need to choose a member of your entourage to help you with this trick. Since it involves shuffling the cards, it is best to avoid a Captain Hook lookalike. Take two packs of cards with different designs on the back so that one pack is distinguishable from the other. Give one pack to your assistant and tell him (for the purposes of the performance, we'll assume your assistant is male) to copy every move you make. You can take this to extremes and have him licking the end of his nose or scratching his bottom (this being another reason for not choosing someone with a metal hook for a right hand). Shuffle the cards and, while your assistant is busy shuffling, sneak a look at the bottom card of your deck. You then swap packs and ask him to pick a card from his deck. It is here that you announce grandly that you are going to read his mind by selecting exactly the same card from your pack. This assertion will inevitably be greeted with much scoffing and ridicule, but you press on unbowed. Pick your card, but don't let him see what it is. Replace your chosen card on top of your pack and tell him to do the same. Now both cut your cards and swap packs again. You know that the card he chose will be immediately under the one you saw earlier at the base of your pack. Tell him to pull out the chosen card from his pack and lay it on the table. You pick out the card which is under the sneak-look card and, as if by magic, they're the same. You must be a mind-reader...

Elevenses

🦉 Skill Level: ❺

Shuffle the cards and deal out the top 21 alternately in three columns of seven. Ask your volunteer to choose a card from any of the three columns, to remember it and put it back in the same place. Ascertain which of the three columns the chosen card is in and gather up the columns, ensuring that the one containing the chosen card is in the middle. Deal the 21 cards out again in the same way, asking your volunteer to tell you which column the card is in. Once again pick up the 21 cards, taking care to put the column containing the selected card in the middle. Repeat the process for a third time, again placing the column with the mystery card in the middle as you pick them up. Finally deal out 11 cards from the top. Turn over the 11th card and, to everyone's surprise (including yours), it will be the chosen card.

The Foretelling

 **Skill Level:** ❺

YOU WILL NEED:
A SHEET OF PAPER, A PEN

Take an ordinary sheet of paper, fold it in half and then fold the top piece back on itself. Over the second fold write in large block letters the number of a playing card, such as 4 OF HEARTS, so that the writing protrudes on either side of the fold. When you open out the paper, you will have two rows of strange hieroglyphics. Add more shapes to the rows to make them look like some obscure Ancient Egyptian scriptures and, for extra authenticity, create a third row of writing between the other two. Place the four of hearts, or whichever card you have written on the paper, on the top of the pack and ask someone to think of a number between one and 10. Deal that number of cards face down from the top of the pack and show the person the bottom card of those dealt. That is his chosen card. It also happens to be the original top card – the four of hearts. Show him the obscure sheet of paper and promise that somewhere in the scrawl is the prediction of the card he would choose. Simply fold the paper so that the two halves of your initial writing are joined together again and sure enough it reads 4 OF HEARTS.

Eights

 **Skill Level: ⑤**

For this trick, you need to arrange the pack so that the four eights are in 10th, 20th, 30th and 40th position. Ask someone to choose a number between 10 and 20. If the number is 18, deal 18 cards face down, then say: "18 is 1 and 8. 1 and 8 is 9." At this, you deal eight cards back on to the pack, placing the ninth card face down to one side. Ask for another number between 10 and 20. For 13, deal 13 cards face down and after your little speech about 1 and 3 making 4, deal three cards back on to the pack and put the fourth face down to one side. Repeat this manoeuvre twice more so that you have four cards face down in a row. Remind your volunteer that all the numbers were chosen completely at random and then turn over the four cards. Unless your ability to add up has deserted you, they will be the four eights.

Double Discovery

Skill Level: ⑤

This is another one of those tricks where the secret is in the preparation. The pack of cards is divided into two halves. One half contains all the odd-numbered red cards and all the even-numbered black cards (jacks count 11, queens 12 and kings 13). In the other half are all the even-numbered red cards and odd-numbered black cards. In finest magician mode, call for two volunteers to help you with this trick. Each volunteer is handed half of the pack to shuffle, the mix of cards in their grasp seemingly being so random (with cards of all four suits, high and low) as to convince them that there is no chicanery afoot. Tell them to select a card, memorize it and place it face-down among the cards held by the other volunteer. Further convince them that everything is above board by allowing them to shuffle their half as often as they like. Still keeping the two halves separate, ask the two volunteers to try and find the other person's chosen card which, unless they have got a Saturday job as a mind-reader or have read this book, they will be unable to do. Then calmly, but not too arrogantly, announce that you will do it for them. As you scan each pre-arranged half, it is easy for your trained eye to spot the interloper because it doesn't fit in with the odd-even, red-black sequence. Remove the offending card from each half and lay them face down on the table. Ask the volunteers to name their cards and, with a flourish, turn over the two cards on the table to reveal that they are the chosen pair.

Name That Card

Skill Level: ⑥

This trick is more a test of stamina than magic. Shuffle the cards, deal them face down into four piles of 13 and ask someone to think of any card. Pick up one of the stacks, fan the cards out and ask whether the mystery card is among them. If necessary, repeat this procedure with the other three stacks until the card is located. Please note that the person merely has to acknowledge the presence of the card – they must not blurt out, "yes, that's it, the four of clubs". When the card has been spotted, gather up the four stacks, making sure that the one containing the mystery card is the top stack so that you know that the card is among the top 13 in the pack. Once again deal the cards face down into four piles. Now you know that the card will be one of the three or four cards at the bottom of one of the piles. Fan the stacks as before. When you learn which stack the card is in, place that stack under the other three as you form them into a pack. Yet again deal the cards face down into four stacks so that the card will be at the top of one of the stacks. Fan the cards as before and, when you are told which stack the mystery card is in, put that stack face down on the table. Pick up one of the other stacks, sneaking a look at the bottom card as you do so. Put that stack on top of the one with the sought-after card. Put these two stacks on top of the remaining cards. Ask your patient volunteer (who by now is probably in pyjamas) to cut the cards a couple of times. Finally look through the cards, find the card you glimpsed and the card the person has been thinking of all this time will be the one above it.

Rows Of Five

Skill Level: ⑥

Shuffle the pack and deal out 25 cards face up in five rows of five. Ask someone to concentrate silently on one of the cards and to tell you which row that card is in. You must then make a mental note of the card at the left end of that row. This will be your key card. Next you collect the cards, beginning with the card at the far right end of the bottom row and working upwards. When you reach the top of that column, go back down to the bottom of the next column along and continue in this way until you have gathered up all 25 cards. When you have done that, once again deal the cards face up into five rows. Locate your key card and ask which row the chosen card is in now. His card will be in the same column as the key card and, since you now know the row, you can readily identify the mystery card.

Bottom Shuffle

Skill Level: ❻

After the pack has been thoroughly shuffled in full view of your audience, sneak a look at the bottom card. Holding the pack in your left hand, use your forefinger to pull the bottom card back a little from the front edge of the pack. Keep a firm grip on this card and begin dealing the other cards from the bottom of the pack face up as quickly as you can. While doing this, tell the audience to shout "Stop!" whenever the fancy takes them. At the "Stop!" command, produce the bottom card which you have been keeping back, put it face down on the table and call out what it is. When the card is turned over, they will see that you are right.

All Fours

☝ Skill Level: ⑥

This trick requires the services of four volunteers so it gives you the chance to impress a wider audience with your skills. Give the cards a good shuffle and remove any four. Show these to your first volunteer and ask him to think of one without telling you which it is. Place the cards back on the table aside from the main pack, take out another four from the pack, show them to volunteer number two and ask him to remember any one card. Then put these four cards into a pile on top of the first four. Repeat the process with two more people so that there are 16 cards on the table and each person has remembered a card. Next deal out the cards into four piles of four. Show the cards in all four piles to the first volunteer and ask him to say which pile contains the card he is thinking of. As a result of the way you have re-dealt the cards, his card will be the first in the pile he has indicated. So you can name it with supreme confidence. Do the same with the second person (his card will be the second in the pile he indicates). Similarly the third person's card will be third in the pile he points to and the fourth person's card will be the fourth in the pile he indicates. And even if more than one person happens to name the same pile, the theory remains the same. The first person's card will be first in the pile, the second person's second and so on.

Sticky Fingers

 **Skill Level: ⑥**

YOU WILL NEED:
GLUE

To prepare for this trick, glue two cards together. If you don't want to ruin your pack, choose the jokers, and in any case use a light glue rather than superglue so that you can prise them apart afterwards if necessary. Put the two cards which have been glued together on top of the pack, fan out the cards and ask someone to pick a card and remember it. Your deception can only be uncovered if the person is stupid enough to pick the top card. Have the card replaced on top of the pack so that it is now immediately above the trick card. Cut the cards at random as many times as you wish and flick through the pack until you feel the snap sound that reveals the location of the thick glued card. The chosen card will be the one immediately above it.

Jacks Away

Skill Level: ❻

YOU WILL NEED:
A MATCHSTICK

Prepare the pack so that the four jacks are at the bottom. Hold the pack face down in your left hand (your thumb at one side, your fingers at the other) and ask one of your friends to use a match to push a group of cards a little way out of the pack. Grip the protruding cards between the thumb and forefinger of your right hand, but as you pull them away, use your thumb to slide out the bottom card of the pack too – one of the jacks. Place that pile (with the jack at the bottom) face down on the table. Repeat the process with the match three more times so that you have four heaps and, unbeknown to your audience, a jack at the bottom of each one. Finally you turn over the piles face up to reveal the four jacks.

The Changing of the Card

Skill Level: ⑥

YOU WILL NEED:
GLUE

Choose any three playing cards from the pack and fold two of them exactly in half so that they sit at right angles. Place the vertical pieces of each card back to back and glue them together and then stick the horizontal sections to the face of the third card. The result is a card with a movable flap which reveals one card when the flap is pulled up and a different card when the flap is pushed down. Use this card to baffle your friends by holding it in your left hand face up and then passing your right hand over it and secretly pushing down the flap. You can then, of course, reverse the procedure to reproduce the original card. To make the trick more dramatic, it is best to use two cards of different-coloured suits, say a spade and a diamond. But be warned: some people witnessing the five of spades changing before their very eyes into the 10 of diamonds can react in an alarming way. The next thing you know they're on the phone to Mulder and Scully and recalling the day when aliens descended and snatched Uncle Cyril's false teeth from the glass by the side of his bed.

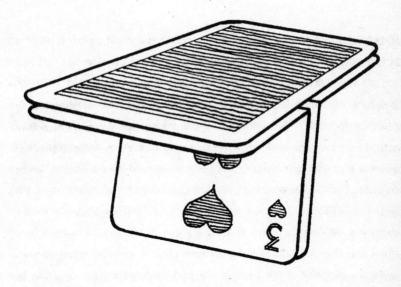

X Ray Eyesight

Skill Level: ⑥

X-ray vision would be a tremendous benefit if you could switch it on or off at will. After all, most of the male population would consider it a real boon for viewing Ulrika Jonsson on "Gladiators", but few would relish the prospect of seeing Michael Fish's cold front while he is delivering the weather forecast. This trick will leave your friends with the distinct impression that you have somehow managed to acquire X-ray eyesight. As you cut the pack, take note of the bottom card, which we'll say is the five of clubs. Put the pack behind your back and switch the bottom card (the five of clubs) so that it is now face up on top of the deck. Show the pack to everyone, holding the cards in such a way that the five of clubs is facing them and they assume that the remaining cards are also facing forward. Stare meaningfully at the back of the pack and declare that you can see straight through to the five of clubs. In fact, you are looking at another card on the bottom of the pack, say the nine of diamonds. Shut your eyes, put the pack behind your back again and move the nine of diamonds face up to the front. Showing the pack to your audience as before, announce that the top card is the nine of diamonds, at the same time making a mental note of the new bottom card. You can carry on like this until everyone is convinced either of your X-ray vision or that you are a brazen cheat.

A Sharp Cut

 **Skill Level: 7**

Fan out the cards, ask one of your disciples to choose one and remember it, and then tell him or her to replace the card face down on top of the pack. You're now going to cut the cards, but the trick is to ramble on in true magician mode so that the audience are concentrating on your face rather than your hands. To perform the sharp cut, you hold the pack with both hands, ensuring that the fingers of your left hand exercise a firm grip on the top card. Still gripping the top card in your left hand, pull out the top half of the deck with your right, except the top card itself which will then slide into place as the top card in your left hand. Put the cards in your right hand under those in your left. You have thus performed a cut without changing the top card. Tap the top of the deck and say that you are going to bring the chosen card back up to the top and when you turn it over, the magic has worked. You can repeat this ruse over and over again – obviously the faster you are able to do it the better – and your audience will never cease to be amazed… although signs of tedium may set in by the third day.

The Lost Card

🎓 Skill Level: ❻

Here you do your best Sherlock Holmes impersonation to track down a missing card. Have the pack shuffled and, by riffling one end with your thumb, sneak a look at the top card. Pass the pack to a member of your entourage and, with your back turned so you can't see what he's doing, tell him to count out as many cards as he wants, to remember the number of cards he has counted and to remember the name of the next card in the pack. So if he has counted out eight cards, he must memorize the ninth card. Get him to replace the cards he has counted on the top of the pack so that they are immediately above the mystery card. Take the pack and seek out the card which you glimpsed at the very start. Remove that card and all the cards behind it and put them at the base of the pack. Hand the pack to your new-found assistant and tell him to count out the same number of cards as he had done previously. Get him to look at the next card and ask him whether it was the same one as the mystery card. When he says no, you have to pretend to look worried. Pick up the card he has just looked at and put it on top of the cards he has counted out. Then put this pile on top of the rest of the pack. Stress that you're not implying he can't count up to eight or whatever, but that you'd like a second opinion. Count out the same number again, turn over the next card and this will indeed be the mystery card. Another successful case has been solved.

The Lady Vanishes

 **Skill Level: 7**

YOU WILL NEED:
SCISSORS, STICKY TAPE, A SPARE QUEEN OF HEARTS

Your first task with this trick is to behead the queen of hearts. Imagine it as Cilla Black in full song and you'll have no problem. Cut the heads from either end of the queen and, with one piece face up and the other face down, join them together at the top using sticky tape as a hinge. Fold the hinged card (with the sticky tape hidden inside, on the back) and slide it over one end of the joker. All of this must be done in secret, away from prying eyes. For the trick itself, you place the imposter queen between two kings, showing the three cards to your audience in such a way that only the very top of the queen is visible. The audience must be able to see that it is a queen, but must not be able to see that from the neck down she is a joker. Close the cards by pressing them down with your finger and hold them face down, making sure that the hinged edge is nearest to you. Take out the bottom card (one of the kings) and place it face down on the table. Carefully place the next card (the joker) face down on the table, keeping the hinged section of queen's heads hidden in your hand. Finally put the last card face down on the table, swap the cards around and ask everyone to

119

guess which card is the queen. While they are doing so, slip the hinged piece into your pocket. Naturally they will be supremely confident of guessing correctly, so watch for the look of disbelief on their faces when you turn it over and they see that it's the joker. Furthermore, the other two cards are revealed to be kings. The lady has vanished. Hitchcock couldn't have done it better.

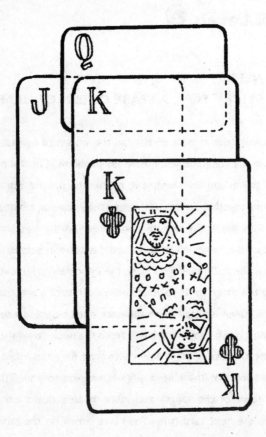

Five Card Choice

Skill Level: ❼

Ask someone to deal you 15 cards. From these cards, pick five which contain a representation of suits — say a club, a diamond, a heart and two spades (if you don't get a decent cross-section, have the cards dealt again). It is important to memorize the order of the suits among the five so arranging them in alphabetical order is a definite help. Ask your friend to make a mental note of any one of the cards and, in addition, remember the last card yourself. Put your five cards in order on top of the pack and place the other 10 on top of them. Now move the top five cards to somewhere in the middle of the pack and then do the same with the bottom five cards. Finally put the new top five cards in the middle so that your original five are now back on top again. Hold those five cards behind your back and ask your friend to reveal his or her chosen card. Since you know the order of the suits and the identity of the last card of the five, you can produce the chosen card from behind your back without even looking.

A Cut Above

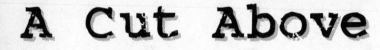 **Skill Level: 7**

YOU WILL NEED:
A HANDKERCHIEF

Make sure you know the identity of the top card in the pack and perform the sharp cut so that it remains on top. Hold the pack face down in your left hand and drape a handkerchief (clean, please!) over the cards. As you do so, secretly turn the pack face up in your hand. In order to conceal your subterfuge, avoid using a see-through handkerchief. Ask someone to cut the pack under the handkerchief and, as what is thought to be the top half is lifted and set aside, turn the cards in your hand over again. After all the cutting, the top card will be the same card as at the start of the trick. Ask your friend to look at the top card without showing you. He or she thinks that card has been cut at random whereas you know it has all been carefully arranged. Put both halves of the pack back together and have them shuffled thoroughly. Deal out the cards face up, announcing that you will stop at the card which your friend has chosen. To inject a little drama and give false hope to any doubters, you can deliberately go past the card before doubling back to it.

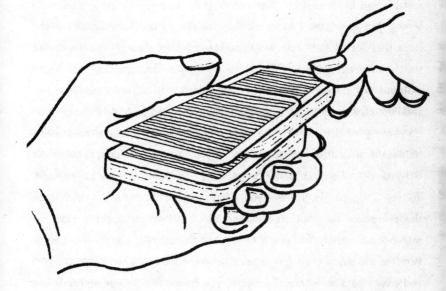

Lucky Number

Skill Level: ❼

Magicians can bring out the worst in human behaviour. Sometimes we only watch them in anticipation that one of their illusions will go spectacularly wrong. Just as we used to sit through ice skating on "Grandstand" in the hope that Torvill and Dean would suddenly plunge through the ice, so we watch magicians on live TV on the off-chance that one day the dutiful assistant will stagger out of the metal booth with a sword between her shoulder-blades, followed by a posse of elderly St John Ambulance men clambering frantically on to the stage to usher an early commercial break. Whilst this trick does not offer the same prospect of bloodshed (a paper cut from the jack of clubs is hardly comparable), it is one where you can pretend, Tommy Cooper-style, that everything has gone horribly wrong. It relies upon the sharp cut demonstrated earlier. Ask a friend to select a card, to memorize it without showing it to you and to replace it on top of the pack. Perform the sharp cut a few times to make it look as if the cards are well and truly mixed up whereas, provided you have done the cut correctly, the same card will still be on top. Then ask for a number between two and 10 and deal out the corresponding number of cards face down. If the number is six, deal six cards. In a state of blind panic, confess that you've forgotten the magic word and will be forced to abandon the trick. Gather up the six cards in order and put them back on top of the pack, the mystery card now being sixth from the top. Suddenly inspiration comes and you say you've remembered the magic word. Count out the chosen number of cards again (in this case, six) and your friend's original card will be the last one.

The Rising Card

 **Skill Level:** ❼

YOU WILL NEED:
SCISSORS

The only drawback to this trick is that it requires the wholesale destruction of your pack of cards. If you want to split hairs, it's actually only half of the pack which is butchered, but you can't have much of a game with 26 cards. It's like playing Happy Families with some of the cards missing, when you end up with Mrs Bun the single parent or Master Chop the orphan. To make this trick work, you need to cut a hole in the back of 26 of the cards. The hole should be near the base of the card, in an identical position on each one and large enough to accommodate your forefinger with a little to spare. Divide the pack into two – in one face-down pile are the 26 cut cards below an ordinary card, and in the other pile are the 25 remaining intact cards. Ask someone to choose a pile. If he chooses the genuine half, let him take it; if he chooses the holey half, pick it up and give him the other half. Either way you can't lose. That's the beauty of being a magician. Ask him to select a card from the ordinary half and to replace it in the other half which you are holding in your hand. Place the cut half on top of the ordinary half and turn the pack face up. Remove the bottom card, which was originally the uncut card on top of the fake pile, and put it somewhere in the ordinary

125

half. Pick the cards up, square them and hold the pack out in front of you so that the audience can only see the face of the top card. Make sure that nobody can see the back of the pack. Grip the pack with your thumb on one side and three fingers on the other, leaving your forefinger free to probe the hole in the top card. Poke your finger through the tunnel formed by the holes in the cards until you come to a barrier. This will be the sought-after card. When you reach it, force it up with your finger so that it magically rises out of the pack.

Telephone Directory

Skill Level: 7

YOU WILL NEED:
A TELEPHONE DIRECTORY, A HANDKERCHIEF,
A PIECE OF PAPER, A PENCIL

Flick through the phone directory and find someone with a silly name –
Blackadder, Snogworthy, Irritable-Bowel or Tibballs. Make a note of the
page number and line number and choose the corresponding cards from
the pack. So if it's page 79, line 18, choose a seven, a nine, an ace and an
eight; if it's page 147, line 26, choose an ace, a four, a seven, a two and a
six. After writing the chosen name on a piece of paper, which should then
be placed in your pocket, place the cards in order on top of the pack. In
the first instance (page 79, line 18), the seven would be on top, the nine
would be the second card, the ace would be the third card and the eight
would be the fourth card. Now for the trick. Tell your friend that you will
somehow predict which name they are going to choose from the entire
local phone directory. Add that their choice will be made via a random
selection of cards. Place the cards face down in your left hand and cover
them with a handkerchief. Repeat the skill demonstrated in "A Cut Above",
whereby you turn the pack over beneath the handkerchief, get your friend
to lift off the 'top' half of the pack and set it aside and then you craftily turn
the cards in your hand face down again. The net result of all this activity is

that the top card is the same as when you started. Ask your friend to take the top two cards from those in your hand (if it's a three-digit page number, it will need to be the top three cards). In this example, it will be a seven and a nine. Tell them to turn to page 79 of the directory. Then ask them to take the next two cards from the pack – the ace and the eight – and to go down 18 lines on page 79. Ask them to read out the name on line 18 and at the same time produce the piece of paper correctly predicting the chosen name.

Changing Aces

Skill Level: ❼

Take the four aces from the pack with the ace of clubs on top, followed by the ace of hearts, the ace of diamonds and the ace of spades. Keep the cards face down. Close the cards, place them in your left hand and, as described earlier, lift off the top two cards as if they were one. Show everyone what they think is the top card – the red ace of hearts – then craftily put the real top card – the ace of clubs – face down on the table. Next reverse count the remaining three aces into your right hand so that the other black ace – the ace of spades – is now on top. Using the same double lift method, show the audience what they believe is the new top card – the red ace of diamonds – but instead deal the real top card – the ace of spades – on to the table. The audience think the two red aces have been dealt on to the table but, when you turn the cards over, they are the two black aces. The red and black cards have magically changed places.

Dancing Queens

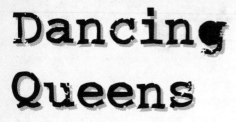 **Skill Level: 7**

YOU WILL NEED:
A SPARE JACK OF SPADES, TWO BOXES, SCISSORS, GLUE

Since this trick requires the destruction of four cards, it is best to use an old pack, or better still, someone else's. To prepare, you need to glue the queen of spades and the jack of spades back to back. Then glue the back of the queen of clubs on to the face of the queen of spades, but a third of the way along so that they appear side by side. Trim the overlapping edge of the queen of clubs so that it is the same size as the queen of spades underneath. Next glue the back of the spare jack of spades to the face of the cut queen of clubs, again about a third of the way along. Trim the overlapping edge of the jack to the size of the queen of spades. You now have a normal-sized playing card with the jack of spades on one side and a third each of the queen of spades, queen of clubs and jack of spades on the other. Begin the trick by showing the audience two empty boxes. Let them have a good look so that they can see there are no secret flaps or compartments. Pick up a perfectly ordinary jack of clubs and hold it in your hand next to the montage card – when you show these to the audience, it looks as if you are holding four cards. Drop the cards into one of the boxes, but then declare your intention of removing the jack of spades. Pick up the special card and show the audience the face where only the jack of spades is visible. Make sure that nobody sees the cut and paste card on the reverse side. Drop the jack of spades into the second box. Next transfer the normal jack of clubs into the second box. Everyone will think that you've swapped the two jacks into the second box, leaving behind the two queens in the first box. But now you show them the first box and, incredibly, the two queens have done a runner. Furthermore when you go the second box and hold up the cards as before, showing two queens and two jacks, it can be seen that the queens have somehow danced across from one box to the other. Cue applause.

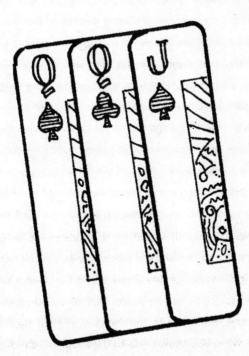

Mystic Leg

 **Skill Level: 7**

YOU WILL NEED:
A PIECE OF PAPER, A PEN

This exhibition of uncanny prediction begins with you writing "Your chosen card is the four of spades" on a piece of paper. Slip the paper down your sock – somewhere there is no chance of it being discovered (for weeks if need be) – and put the four of spades face down on top of the pack. Holding the pack behind your back, cunningly slide the top card off and slip it into the waistband of your trousers. Make sure you're not wearing baggy trousers or it could necessitate an unseemly strip to retrieve the four of spades. Give the rest of the pack to your friend and ask for the cards to be shuffled and handed back to you. Once again, hold the cards behind your back and coolly lift the four of spades from your waistband and put it back on top of the deck. Ask your friend to take the top card, to remember it and to put it back anywhere in the deck. Scan the cards and confidently take out any card except the four of spades. With a certain air of smugness (not an altogether alien trait in some magicians), say: "Is this your card?" With great relish, your friend (perhaps soon to become your ex-friend) will snarl: "No, you've got it wrong. I knew you couldn't do it. It was the four of spades." But he who laughs last, laughs after he who laughs first or whatever it is. Still feigning dejection, reach into your sock and produce the piece of paper bearing the words: "Your chosen card is the four of spades." Gobsmacked doesn't begin to describe it.

The Four Aces

Skill Level: ❽

The most baffling card tricks are the ones where your friends do all the work, thus apparently leaving no room for you to manipulate the pack. The key to this piece of deception is to have all four aces on top of the pack at the start. You can of course cut the pack to show good faith but, in doing so, perform the sharp cut so that the aces remain on top. Put the pack down and ask someone to cut the cards into four piles. Beginning with the pile on the left, being the pile furthest from the one with the aces at the top, ask for the cards to be mixed up by switching the top three cards of the pile to the bottom. Then ask for the next three cards on that same pile to be distributed one each on top of the other three piles. Ask for the left-hand pile to be put back. Have the same procedure repeated with the three remaining piles – top three cards to the bottom, next three cards on top of each of the other piles. Ask everyone whether they are happy that the cards have been well and truly mixed up. They will almost certainly all say "yes" (anybody perverse enough to say "no" should simply be ignored) whereupon you turn over the top card on each of the four piles to reveal that they are the four aces.

The Final Card

Skill Level: ⑧

This one's a corker. Take a well shuffled pack and sneak a look at the bottom card. Ask a friend to take a card and to remember it without telling you. Cut the pack and tell him to place his card on the top half, then lay the bottom half on top of that. Cut the pack a couple of times and then search through the cards, ostensibly in a hunt for his card, but what you're really looking for is the card that was on the bottom. When you find it, cut the cards again so that it reverts to its position at the base of the pack. It's play-acting time again, that time in a trick when you are overcome by gloom and despondency. You can't find his card, you whimper plaintively. Perhaps a tear starts to trickle down your cheek... particularly if he's just poked you in the eye because he's waiting to get down to the pub. Search through the pack once more, this time silently counting out 21 cards from the bottom. With another despairing shake of the head (people have won Oscars for less!), put the 21 cards on the top of the pack and announce that you'll have to resort to plan B. This involves dealing out all 52 cards into two piles (deal to your friend first). At the end of the deal, ask whether the card he chose is in his pack. He should say no (if not, it's back to the drawing-board), in which case you discard his half and deal out the remaining 26 in two piles. Carry on dealing like this until you are left with one card. Turn it over and it will be the card he chose.

The Short Card Trick

 **Skill Level:** ❽

YOU WILL NEED:
SCISSORS

This trick operates on the same principle as "The Final Card", but involves the creation of what is known in magic circles as a "short card". To make a short card, you need to trim the top edge by about an eighth of a centimetre. This might not sound much, but when the pack is squared off neatly the short card is immediately identifiable to the magician and can thus serve as a key card to help with locating others. The amount cut off is so small that the audience can spot nothing untoward, even in close-up. Short cards may be used in all manner of tricks. Here you have to prepare the pack so that the short card is the 22nd card from the top. Spread the cards and allow your volunteer to pick one. While he is studying his chosen card (it's amazing how long it takes some people to remember the seven of diamonds), flick through the pack with your fingertips so that you can locate the short card. If he has selected a card from the part of the pack below the short card (cards 23–52, that is), divide the pack immediately above the short card and have the mystery card inserted there. That card now occupies 22nd position. If however he took a card from the part of the pack above the short card, you need to divide the pack at the short card and insert the chosen card immediately below that one to ensure that it is the 22nd card from the top. You now deal out the cards alternately into two piles – the first face up, the second face down. Ask your volunteer to tell you whether his card is in the face-up heap. If you have counted correctly, it won't be. Deal out the face-down pile as before (alternately face up and face down) and continue like this until there is just one card left face down. That will be the mystery card.

The Pair of Aces

Skill Level: 8

For this exercise you need two packs of cards with identical colours and patterns on the back. Before unleashing your magical powers on an unsuspecting public, secretly take the ace of hearts and the ace of diamonds from one pack of cards and put one at each end of the other pack, giving you a pack of 54 cards. You don't need the remaining 50 cards of the first pack. Take the 54-strong pack and hold it in a fan, keeping the backs of the cards facing your audience so that they can't see the two aces at either end. Make a bold show of announcing that you want to find the ace of hearts and the ace of diamonds. Remove the duplicate pair (still leaving you with the aces on the ends) and hold them up so that the audience can see them. Then replace the two aces clearly somewhere in the middle of the pack, close the pack and grip it firmly between your fingers and your thumb. Now comes the tricky bit. Throw the pack to the floor while keeping hold of the two end cards. As the cards cascade downwards, you are left holding the ace of hearts and the ace of diamonds. Show them to the audience... and hope that nobody spots the spare aces lying somewhere in the pile on the carpet.

Hypnosis

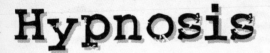 **Skill Level: ⑨**

YOU WILL NEED:
TWO SPARE CARDS, SCISSORS, A PIECE OF ELASTIC
OR A THIN ELASTIC BAND

Take any two cards from a spare pack and make short vertical cuts in the top of both cards. Cut a piece of elastic about 10cm long and tie a knot near each end. Pass the elastic through the slits in the two cards, with the knots at the back, making sure the cards are facing the same way. After all that, you can get down to business. Put the linked cards at the bottom of the pack with the elasticated end nearest you, fan out all of the cards face down and ask somebody to pick one. But, by fair means or foul, steer them clear of the trick cards. Instruct them to remember the card and put it face down on the table. Cut the pack so that the trick cards move to the middle, pick up the chosen card and insert it into the pack in the elastic loop which links the trick cards. As you push the card in, the elastic stretches. Grip the pack firmly and hold it up. Ask your friend to name the chosen card and announce that you are going to hypnotize it into rising out of the pack. Mutter a few words of mystical gibberish, loosen your grip and the card will jump out of the pack.

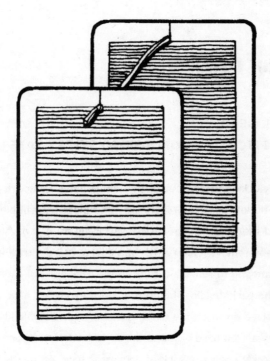

Cascade of Cards

🖐 **Skill Level: ⑨**

YOU WILL NEED:
A SMALL PIECE OF DOUBLE-SIDED STICKY TAPE

The art of plucking a card out of thin air is nobly demonstrated in this spectacular trick. The only preparation is to place a small piece of clear, double-sided sticky tape on the back of your right hand. It might pull on the hairs when you remove it afterwards but, believe me, the trick is worth the pain. Ask someone to select a card from the pack and put it on top of the deck. Cut the pack, holding the bottom half in your left hand and putting the top half face down on the table with your right hand. Suddenly throw the cards in your left hand high into the air and, while everyone is watching them fall, quickly press the back of your right hand on to the pile on the table so that the top card sticks to the adhesive tape. As the cards descend, reach your right hand out into the middle of the cascade and emerge with the chosen card on the back of your hand. Everyone will think you have performed an amazing feat of magic… except the smart Alec who has read books like this and knows to watch your hands instead of the cards.

The Flying Card

Skill Level: ⑩

In this variation of "Cascade of Cards", you ask a volunteer to shuffle the pack, pick a card, memorize it and return it to the top of the deck. Having noted the bottom card as in previous tricks, you can cut the cards and thus know the identity of the secret card. Say that because this is such a top-of-the-bill trick, you need a little more room. As you turn your back on the audience and walk slowly to your new location, find the secret card, slide it to the bottom of the pack and lick your right thumb. Turn round to face your audience once more and, holding the pack with its back to them and with your soggy thumb pressed against the face of the bottom card, throw the entire pack into the air. The bottom card will remain stuck to your thumb and you can reveal that it is indeed the mystery card. With further practice, you will even be able to convey the impression that you have plucked the mystery card out of thin air. As all the cards flutter downwards, you can jab out your arm (the one with the card stuck to the thumb) and everyone will think you have caught the card in flight. It is only when they come to shake you warmly by the hand that they start to wonder where your thumb's been...

The Missing Corner

Skill Level: ⑩

YOU WILL NEED:
A HANDKERCHIEF, AN ELASTIC BAND, A BALL-POINT PEN

The majority of card tricks can be performed just about anywhere (although the cards do tend to get a little soggy in the bath), but this trick is so baffling that it demands a grander backdrop – a smart lounge at the very least. Indeed it is so impressive that you might even care to dress for the occasion. But if you can't find magicians' white gloves, don't try to do it on the cheap with a pair of rubber gloves! As preparation, you need to tear off one corner from any card in the pack, approximately a quarter of the size of the card. Throw that piece away and put the torn card face down on the top of the deck so that the missing quarter is situated at the bottom left-hand corner. Place another card above it on the deck, relegating the torn card to second position. One more thing: you need an elastic band in your right-hand trouser pocket. Now hold the pack face down and ask someone to choose a card. After he has taken his card, put the pack face up on the table and nonchalantly remove the card at the bottom of the deck (this is the one that was earlier hiding the torn card). To justify your action, wave the card in the air, explaining that the person could have picked absolutely any card. Replace this card at the top of the face-up deck. The torn card is therefore now at the bottom. Take the card which your volunteer has chosen and tear off one corner, roughly the same size as you tore from the first card. Make sure that the piece you remove shows both the number and suit of the parent card. Hand the three-quarter section of card to him and ask him to write his initials on it. Holding the pack face down, you then put that card on top of the deck so that it is immediately above the first torn card. However the torn part of the chosen card should be at the top right-hand corner of the pack – in other words, the opposite way round to the card beneath it. Next hand him the piece you tore from the card he selected and ask him to sign that too. While he is preoccupied with doing that, you give the impression of dealing his torn card face down on to the table, but in reality you press your right thumb on the top right-hand corner of the pack and pull out the unsigned torn card from beneath the chosen card. By careful positioning of your hands, make sure that nobody can see that there is still a torn card on top of the deck. Cut the pack so that the signed torn card is safely tucked away somewhere in the middle. The next stage is to pick up the face-down torn card from the table (the one which everyone thinks is the signed card) and to rip it into three pieces, keeping the face of the card hidden from the audience. Take the signed corner of the chosen card and hold it on top of the other three pieces. The only face which will be visible to the audience will be that of the signed card. As far as they are concerned, all four pieces come from the same card. Hold the four pieces aloft in your right hand, drape a handkerchief over them and, under the cover provided, force the signed piece of card upwards so that it protrudes from the rest. With your left hand, grab the signed section through the handkerchief and hide the other pieces in your right hand. Bring your right hand down to your trouser pocket and pull out the elastic band, at the same time depositing there the three pieces of card. Tie the elastic band around the centre of the handkerchief to hold the piece of card in place at the very top (see illustration). Of course, the audience think there are four pieces of card in the handkerchief. Give the handkerchief to your volunteer and ask him to remove the elastic band. To his amazement, he will find only the torn corner which he signed earlier. Then you fan out the pack to produce the rest of his signed card, magically reassembled. When he matches the corner to this card, he will discover that it is a perfect fit. Everyone will be left scratching their heads in wonderment… as long as you haven't got a hole in your trouser pocket.

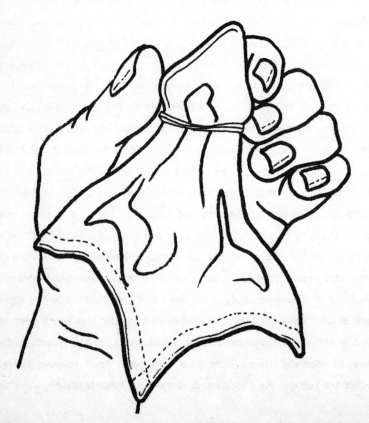

Chapter Three:

Pub Tricks

Different Strokes

 **Skill Level:** ❶

YOU WILL NEED:
PENCIL AND PAPER

This is the easiest trick in the world... once you know how it's done. On a piece of paper, you write six vertical strokes like this: I I I I I I. Challenge anyone to change the six strokes into three without rubbing any of them out, cutting the paper in half or similar cheating. When your friends look at you blankly, like losing finalists at Cruft's, and beg you to tell them the answer, you simply take the pencil and add to the strokes so that you end up with: T H R E E. Annoying, isn't it?

Cross Question

 **Skill Level:** ❶

YOU WILL NEED:
SIX COINS

This is a good trick to sharpen everyone's wits before the pub quiz. Arrange six coins on the table in the shape of a cross — a vertical line of four and one placed either side of the second coin from the top. Tell your friends that, by moving just one coin, they must form two rows with four coins in each. While heads are scratched and brows are furrowed, you can show them how it's done. Simply move the coin at the bottom of the vertical column and place it partly over the coin which is second from the top. You thus make four coins across and four down.

All Square

 **Skill Level:** ❶

YOU WILL NEED:
12 COINS

See whether they have learnt from the previous trick with another simple coin riddle. Arrange 12 coins on the table in a square, four coins on each side, and say that you want the same coins rearranged to form another square, but with five coins on each side. The idea is the same as before. You take one coin from each side and move it to a corner where you stack it partly on top of the coin already there. There are now two coins on each corner, leaving you with five coins on each side.

The Finger
Of Suspicion

Skill Level: ❶

This is really nothing more than a playground joke but, since a lot of pub conversations evoke memories of the fourth form, it is worth including. You tell one of your mates to put his hand flat on the table and then to bend his middle finger back. Now bet him that he can't raise the ring finger of the same hand without moving the other fingers and thumb. No matter how hard he concentrates, he will struggle. And so will everyone else. When hands are aching and fingers are sore, show them what to do. Put your hand flat on the table and bend your middle finger back as ordered before. Then use your other hand to lift the ring finger! Now is probably a good time to nip to the loo.

The X Files

Skill Level: ❶

YOU WILL NEED:
FOUR MATCHES

Arrange four matches on the table in the shape of an X so that there is no space between the four where they meet in the centre. The matches of one arm will be touching, but the other two will be separated by the first two. The join of the two matches which touch should line up with one edge of the other two matches, not the centre of their join. Ask one of your friends to make a square by moving just one match. The words "easy" and "peasy" spring to mind because all you do is pull back the match which touches all three others, so that there is now a tiny square space where the four matches meet in the middle of the X.

Wine Bluff

Skill Level: **1**

YOU WILL NEED:
A BOTTLE OF WINE, A GLASS

If you've forsaken the pub for a wine bar, this challenge should ensure that you don't have to pay for the next bottle. When you're about half-way through the bottle and your glass is partly full, put the cork firmly back in the bottle and bet your friends that they can't drink from the bottle without removing the cork. Most will accept that it is impossible, although hardened drinkers may well opt to tip the bottle upside down and place a gaping mouth under the neck in the forlorn hope that a trickle may slither down the sides of the cork. When everyone has admitted defeat, bet them the next bottle that you can do it. Simply turn the bottle upside down, fill the cavity at the base of the bottle with wine from your own glass and drink from the cavity. No wine will ever have tasted better.

Separation

Skill Level: ❶

YOU WILL NEED:
SALT, PEPPER, A PIECE OF PAPER, A GLASS OF WATER

Normally the amount of enjoyment that can be derived from a cruet set extends no further than using the salt and pepper pots to discuss football tactics. But you can also utilize them to play a neat scientific trick on your friends. Sprinkle roughly equal amounts of salt and pepper on to a slip of paper and mix them together with your finger. Bet everyone that you can separate the salt and the pepper just by one turn of your wrist. Seeing the mixture of salt and pepper, they will probably accept whereupon you take a glass of water, pick up the piece of paper and tip the contents into the glass. The salt will sink to the bottom while the pepper will float on the surface. All that's left to do now is collect your winnings.

The Sum of Life

 **Skill Level:** ❷

YOU WILL NEED:
PENCIL AND PAPER, AN ENVELOPE

Any faint knowledge of mathematical principles seems to desert us in the relaxed atmosphere of the pub, which is how we sometimes forget that a 16-stone thug and seven lagers add up to trouble. So a trick which relies on a fairly simple mathematical theory is unlikely to be challenged by any of your friends who will instead be utterly mesmerized by your remarkable foresight. You start by writing down a number on a piece of paper and getting someone to put it in an envelope and seal it. Allow them to check that there's nothing untoward about the envelope. The number you write should be exactly twice the number of the current year so if you are performing this trick in 1998, you write down 3996. Then call on your friends to choose someone to take part. The end result will seem even more impressive if the volunteer is a person you barely know. Hand the volunteer a pencil and paper and ask him to write down the answers to these four questions:

* **THE YEAR OF HIS BIRTH**
* **THE YEAR HE FIRST STARTED WORK**

* **HIS AGE AT THE END OF THIS YEAR**
* **THE NUMBER OF YEARS SINCE HE STARTED WORK.**

Ask him to add up the four numbers. The total will always be twice the current year, so when your volunteer opens the sealed envelope to reveal your prediction, the two figures will tally.

Fraud!

Skill Level: ❶

YOU WILL NEED:
A COIN, A HANDKERCHIEF

For the best results, perform this piece of financial deception after you've done a few other coin tricks. Provided you haven't made a hash of the previous tricks, your friends will grudgingly admit that you do have some vague idea as to what you're doing and therefore they won't suspect that you will stoop as low as this. Success depends entirely on an accomplice. You start by placing a coin in the palm of your hand. Partly close your hand, turn it over and cover it with a handkerchief. Then ask all of your friends (if you keep playing tricks on them, you probably haven't got many) to step forward and feel the coin in your hand. The last person to come forward must be your accomplice who, instead of just touching the coin, removes it. You then toss away the handkerchief with a theatrical flourish and reveal your hand to be empty. People used to be burnt at the stake for less...

Three Squares

Skill Level: ❷

YOU WILL NEED:
EIGHT MATCHES

There is always a tremendous sense of anticipation associated with the first pint of the day. You get down to the pub for opening time, with a throat like sandpaper, and you watch the barman pull that first heavenly pint. And what happens? There is a violent gurgling sound and what should be something approaching amber nectar comes out looking like the product of a rabid dog. You have a pint of foam, at which point the barman suggests that the lager may need changing. While he sets off to do his duty, you are left in limbo. Anticipation has turned to frustration. By now, there are two or three other customers in the same boat, all equally impatient. To keep tempers under control and to pass the time while waiting for the barman to return, demonstrate a quick trick. Challenge anyone to make three squares from just eight matches. It will be just your luck if the guy next to you has seen the trick before, in which case it will take him approximately 10 seconds to lay out the matches in two squares, but so that they overlap, thereby forming a third smaller square. Well, it was worth a try…

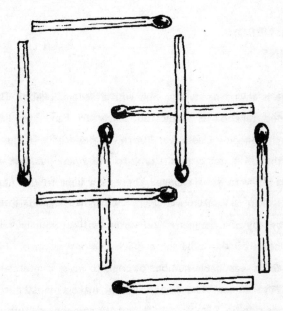

Heads or Tails

Skill Level: ❷

YOU WILL NEED:
SOME COINS

Loose change is always handy in a pub with a decent jukebox. But if the aforementioned jukebox is dedicated solely to Pan Pipe Favourites (including such pan pipe classics as "Born To Be Wild", "Paranoid" and "Anarchy in the UK"), not only is it time to find a new pub, but you need something to do with your change. There is a limit to the number of packets of chicken tikka flavoured crisps which you can devour in one evening. So, by way of a change (no pun intended), get your friends to put some loose coins on the table for a quick demonstration of "Heads or Tails". You need a reasonable number of coins to make it interesting – say half a dozen. After the coins have been laid out, make a mental note of how many are heads side up. Turn your back and ask someone to turn over any even number of coins. He can do this more than once in an attempt to confuse you, but he must never turn over a single coin. Then ask him to cover any one coin with his hand. When you turn back to face the table, you are immediately able to tell him whether the coin under his hand is a head or a tail. The rule is simple. If the number of heads at the start was odd and is still odd now – or was even at the start and is still even – then the covered coin is a tail. However if the number of heads at the start was even but is now odd, or vice-versa, then the hidden coin must be a head. Everybody will be so impressed they won't notice you pocketing the props.

Something Up Your Sleeve

 **Skill Level: ❷**

YOU WILL NEED:
FOUR MATCHBOXES, AN ELASTIC BAND

Despite protestations to the contrary, magicians always seem to have something up their sleeve – whether it be a string of silk scarves, a flock of doves or a herd of wildebeest. The object here is marginally less exciting – a half-full matchbox – but the result can still be amusing. The matchbox is hidden up your right sleeve, tied to your wrist with an elastic band. You start the trick by putting three empty matchboxes on the table. You shake each box in turn – two with your left hand which produces no sound – and the other with your right hand. As a result of the hidden box, when you shake your right armm the audience hears the sound of matches. You then swiftly jumble up the boxes and ask any of the spectators to identify the box which contains the matches. Only you know that they are all empty. When their efforts meet with abject failure, you shake the three boxes again – two with your left hand and one with your right – before mixing them up once more... and so it goes on. Their attempts to find the right box will continue to prove spectacularly unsuccessful until they work out that you really do have something up your sleeve.

Matching Shapes

 **Skill Level:** ❷

YOU WILL NEED:
12 MATCHES

Arrange a dozen matches in a block of four squares as shown. Challenge your friends to remove any two matches so that they leave exactly two squares. You simply remove two of the inner matches so that you are left with one large square and a smaller square within.

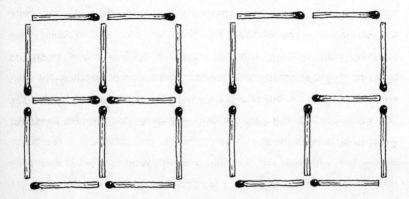

Three Blind Dice

 **Skill Level:** ❷

YOU WILL NEED:
THREE DICE

Even with your back turned, you are able to calculate a player's dice throws. Turn away from the table, ask him to roll three dice and to add up the total, keeping the figure to himself. Let's assume he threw 6, 4, 1 and ended up with 11. Tell him to turn any one of the dice upside down and to add that number to the total. We'll say he turned over the 6 to get a 1 and so his running total is 12. Again he mustn't tell you the score. Ask him to roll the same dice again and to add that new number to his total. If he rolls a 5, his grand total will be 17 although the dice on the table (5, 4 and 1) only add up to 10. You now turn back to face the table with no knowledge of what numbers he threw on his first and second goes. But by adding up the dice in front of you (10) and adding 7, you will always come up with his secret grand total, in this case 17.

Dotto

🦉 Skill Level: ❷

YOU WILL NEED:
PENCIL AND PAPER

As a nation, we love a bet. We'll bet on anything – that the Loch Ness Monster will be discovered before Scotland win the World Cup; that the Teletubbies will split up this year, citing artistic differences; and that Elvis will eventually be discovered hiding away somewhere he thought no one would find him – working as Director of Tourism for a small Midlands town. So the moment you say, "I bet you can't…", you are assured of any number of takers. For this bet, you need a pencil and a piece of paper, the challenge being to draw a circle with a dot in the middle without taking the tip of the pencil off the paper. There will probably be all manner of squiggles as people try and fail, but the solution is quite simple really. You draw your circle in a corner of the paper and leave the pencil tip on the circumference of the circle. With your other hand, you fold over the corner of the paper into a triangular shape so that the point reaches the centre of the circle. Finally you retrace the pencil's journey around part of the circumference and then go across the folded triangle of paper and make a dot next to the point. When you pull back the fold, you have a circle with a dot in the middle and your pencil never once left the paper.

The Changing Triangle

 **Skill Level: ❷**

YOU WILL NEED:
10 COINS

For this coin puzzle, you arrange 10 coins in a triangle – one at the top, two on the second row, three on the third and four at the bottom. The object of the exercise is to turn the triangle upside down by moving only three of the coins. First you move the top coin down to a position beneath the middle two coins on the bottom row. You then move the coin at either end of the old bottom row up two rows and the result is an inverted triangle.

Beer Mat Balance

 **Skill Level:** ❸

YOU WILL NEED:
TWO BEER MATS, A GLASS

This one will bemuse even the most cynical of observers... for at least a minute. To prepare for it, take two identical beer mats, both of which should be in pristine condition. Score one mat from top to bottom down the middle with a penknife. Glue half of the face of that mat to the back of the other mat. Allow the unstuck half to lie flat against the back of the mat in front. Now announce that you are going to balance an ordinary glass on an ordinary beer mat. Hold the mat at the unstuck side and show everyone the back and front. They should all think there is just one mat. With the audience in front of you, place the glass on the top edge of the mat, at the same time pulling out the flap at the back so that it forms a right angle with the rest of the mat. This creates a platform on which the glass can balance. At first, appear reluctant to let go of the glass for fear that it will fall, but eventually pluck up courage and allow the glass to stand unaided. They will all think you've performed a miracle until they insist on inspecting the mat a little more closely, so don't perform this trick more than once to the same circle of friends. It is also advisable to use an empty glass for this trick as a full one might prove too heavy for the card and not only will you incur the wrath of the landlord, more importantly you'll lose your drink.

Secrets

 **Skill Level:** ❸

YOU WILL NEED:
A POCKET CALCULATOR, PENCIL AND PAPER

Warning: This trick could be dangerous. Take care!

There are two things a woman likes to keep secret – her age and the number of men she's slept with – so to prise such information from her is a veritable feat. Here's how it's done. Hand her a pocket calculator and ask her to key in the number of men she's slept with over the years. Tell her to multiply this figure by two, add five and multiply the total by 50. She should then add her age to the total, add 365 and subtract 615. This will leave a final sum which should be written on a piece of paper and handed to you. Unravelling the secrets is now easy for you. The last two numbers in the final total are her age and the preceding figures are the number of men she admits to having slept with. An eight-digit calculator should suffice for this task, but if you're dealing with someone who has led a particularly colourful life you may need a larger model.

Tug o' Napkin

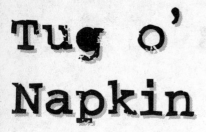

 **Skill Level: ❸**

YOU WILL NEED:
A PAPER NAPKIN

Hang Tough, Pyramid, Run the Gauntlet... Pull the Napkin? No, somehow trying to pull a paper napkin in half is unlikely to earn a place among the tests of strength on "Gladiators", but it requires more physical exertion than you think... unless, of course, you know the secret. Take an ordinary paper napkin, twist it diagonally from one corner to another and roll it tightly so that you end up with something resembling a piece of rope. Challenge any of your friends to break it in half by pulling both ends simultaneously. Hard though they may try, it will all be to no avail. Some egos may even be damaged beyond repair. While everyone's eyes are on macho men being reduced to quivering wrecks by a mere paper napkin, secretly wet your fingers. Now you can step in. Place your wet fingers over the centre of the napkin, an action which has the immediate effect of weakening it. Once the water has taken hold, it is a simple task to pull the napkin apart at that point. Nobody will ever kick sand in your face again.

The Travelling Coin

 **Skill Level:** ❸

YOU WILL NEED:
TWO SMALL COINS

For this trick, the sheer speed of movement deceives the eye. You start with your hands placed on the table, palms upwards, slightly less than a foot apart. On each hand rests a small coin. On the left hand, it is placed in the centre of your palm, but on the right hand, it is situated at the base of the first and second fingers. This positioning is essential, otherwise the trick won't work. Without raising your hands from the table, swiftly turn both hands over and inwards. This movement has the effect of throwing the coin from the right hand over to the left where it is caught by the left hand as it hits the table. Unless you are particularly clumsy, the speed of the transfer will be too quick for the naked eye. Then you ask your spectators to tell you how many coins are under each hand, and they should say one. You promptly astound them by revealing two coins under your left hand and none under your right. If you are left-handed, you will probably find it easier to swap things around by putting one coin in the palm of your right hand and the other at the base of the first two fingers of your left hand so that the coin travels from left to right.

Dice Challenge

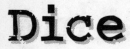 **Skill Level:** ❸

YOU WILL NEED:
TWO DICE

Turn your back on the table and ask one of your mates to throw two dice without telling you the numbers. Let's say he throws 6 and 2. Now tell him to double the number on one of the dice (if he chooses the 6, that's 12), to add 5 (that makes 17), multiply the answer by 5 (giving a total of 85) and then to add the number on the other dice (2). So he ends up with 87. Ask him to subtract 25 and to tell you the resulting number (62). This figure denotes the numbers on the dice he originally threw – 6 and 2 – which means you've worked out what he rolled with your back turned throughout.

Topple the Bottle

🦉 **Skill Level:** ❸

YOU WILL NEED:
A BOTTLE, A PAPER BAG

When you've exhausted every possible topic of conversation – football, music, politics, football, "Coronation Street", religion, football, the history of Pot Noodle, the 10 best places where you've thrown up, and football – here's a trick guaranteed to breathe life into a flagging evening. Produce an empty bottle from a paper bag – everyone had been wondering why you had been carrying them around all evening – stand the bottle on the table and the bag to one side and invite anyone to try and blow over the bottle. Their efforts will result in nothing more than sheer exhaustion which is when you step in to show them how it's done. Stand the bottle on the corner of the paper bag and blow into the bag. As the bag inflates, it knocks over the bottle. With everyone looking disgusted, it will be only a matter of seconds before someone asks: "So who do you fancy for the FA Cup?"

Pocket Money

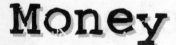 **Skill Level:** ❸

YOU WILL NEED:
A POCKET CALCULATOR, PENCIL AND PAPER

By doing this mathematical challenge, you can find out whether someone has enough money in their pocket to buy the next round. Actually, unless their idea of a round is a packet of crisps split four ways, the answer will be no because the trick only works on sums under £1. It operates on the same principle as "Secrets". Tell your friend to write down his age, double it, add five and multiply by 50. Next he must subtract 365 and add the amount of change in his pocket, in pence. If he is 28 and has 75p, this will give a grand total of 2760. Now you take over by adding 115 to give a final figure of 2875. The first two digits represent his age and the last two denote the amount of change in his pocket. The formula will always work as long as your friend isn't too rich.

Guess the Number

 **Skill Level: ❸**

YOU WILL NEED:
A SET OF DOMINOES

More fun with dominoes! What more could you want from life? Unlike most tricks, this one begins with a visit to the loo. No, you're not going to make all the toilet paper disappear out of the men's cubicle – that's probably been done already – nor are you going to make the hand drier operate at a temperature where it doesn't barbecue your skin. Instead quietly announce that you're just going off to answer a call of nature and, in your absence, you want one of your friends to pick a domino from the set and to put the rest of the set back in the box, hidden from view. When you come back, there is no possible way you can know which domino has been chosen. Yet, without peeking, you are going to name that domino. It's a bit of a struggle at first, so tell whoever chose it that he is going to have to do a quick sum. Get him to look at the higher of the two numbers on the domino (if it's a double, then obviously either number will do) and to multiply it by five. He must then add seven and double the answer. Next he must add on the lower of the two numbers on the domino and subtract 14. The two-digit answer will be the numbers on the mystery domino. So if the domino is 5:1, it works like this: $5 \times 5 = 25 + 7 = 32 \times 2 = 64 + 1 = 65 - 14 = 51$. The numbers are 5 and 1.

The Empty Glass

Skill Level: ❸

YOU WILL NEED:
FOUR MATCHES, A COIN

Arrange four matches into the shape of a wine glass (see illustration) and place a coin between the two vertical matches which form the sides of the "glass". Challenge any of your friends to move the "glass" in such a way that the coin finishes up outside it. Only two matches may be moved. The first move is to slide the horizontal match (the one forming the base of the "glass") half its length to the left. The second move is to switch the detached vertical match (the one which originally formed the right-hand side of the "glass") down to below the left-hand end of the horizontal match. The "glass" is now upside down and the coin is outside.

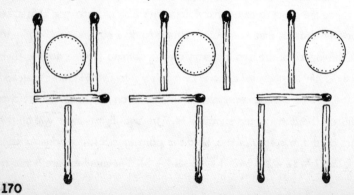

X Static

 **Skill Level: ❸**

YOU WILL NEED:
A £1 COIN, A MATCH, A PLASTIC COMB

Stand a pound coin on its edge on the table and balance a match across the top of the coin. The aim is to move the match off the coin without touching either object. To do this, you need to create static electricity. Rub a plastic comb through your hair or on to the sleeves of your pullover if it's made of wool. Hold the comb next to the match and the static electricity from the comb will cause the match to drop off the coin.

Playing With Fire

 **Skill Level: ❸**

YOU WILL NEED:
A LIGHTED CIGARETTE, AN ICE CUBE

Warning: This trick could be dangerous. Take care!

Why do people choose to eat fire for a living? After all, career openings are rather limited. As a result of government cutbacks, most councils no longer even have a fire-eating department. Yet we still marvel at those who appear to swallow fire without burning away the insides of their mouth. Fire is exceedingly dangerous and is definitely not something to be toyed with, but you can demonstrate your ability to defy pain in a relatively innocuous way which you should be able to perform without having the pub evacuated. Pick up a lighted cigarette and hold the burning tip between your fingers for a few seconds. Do not let anyone take a puff. You should be able to do this without suffering any adverse effects. The secret is that just beforehand you have placed those same fingers on an ice cube or something equally cold. This serves to numb the pain. Now you can pass the lighted cigarette to the next brave contestant while you move on to the bed of nails.

The Domino Effect

Skill Level: ❸

YOU WILL NEED:
A SET OF DOMINOES, A BAG, PENCIL AND PAPER, AN
ENVELOPE

The game of dominoes has undergone something of a renaissance in recent years, and is no longer played solely by men who wear cloth caps and race whippets. This trick with dominoes is deceptively simple, but is guaranteed to impress anyone who knows nothing at all about the game. To set up the trick, you must secretly remove any domino except a double. If the one you pick is 3:2, you then write 3 and 2 on a piece of paper and pop it in a sealed envelope. Begin the performance by handing the envelope to one of your friends, along with a bag full of dominoes (minus, of course, the one you have already taken out). Tell him to set the dominoes out on the table in game fashion, but don't let him count the tiles in case he discovers your villainy. Announce that the envelope contains a prediction as to which numbers will be at either end of the line when all of the tiles have been laid out correctly. When he finishes, ask him to open the envelope and, sure enough, the numbers on the piece of paper will be those at either end of the row – in this case 3 and 2.

Bridge Building

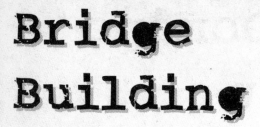 **Skill Level: ❸**

YOU WILL NEED:
A PIECE OF THICK PAPER, THREE GLASSES

Stand two empty glasses of the same height on the table and cover them with a piece of strong paper – something like blotting paper. You then boast that you can perch a third empty glass upright on the paper bridge, thus creating a pyramid shape, but the question is: can anyone else? No matter how carefully they position the glass, the paper will give way, so make sure someone is on hand to catch the falling glass. Alternatively, use a plastic glass – one of those awful things you get in downmarket clubs. It still won't balance, but it will prevent everyone being covered in broken glass. Finally you show them how it's done. Take the piece of paper and fold it several times lengthwise so that you form a row of pleats. Put this on top of the two glasses and then balance the third glass on the corrugated paper. This time it will hold.

Bottle It

Skill Level: ❸

YOU WILL NEED:
AN EMPTY BOTTLE, A BANKNOTE, A PENCIL

If you should ever find yourself in a life-or-death situation where your only hope of salvation is to remove a banknote from beneath an upside down bottle without lifting the bottle, remember this trick. Place the banknote on the table and stand the inverted bottle on top of the note. Lay a pencil across the end of the note nearest to you and roll the note around the pencil towards the bottle, keeping the roll as tight as possible. The note will edge towards you and eventually slide out from under the bottle which remains perfectly upright. As you become increasingly adept at this trick, you will probably be able to dispense with the pencil altogether. But always carry one with you… just in case.

10 Into Five Will Go

 **Skill Level:** ❸

YOU WILL NEED:
A PIECE OF PAPER, PENCIL, SCISSORS,
A 5P COIN, A 10P COIN

Place a 5p coin in the centre of a square piece of paper and draw a line around the circumference of the coin. Cut out the hole which should therefore be exactly the same size as the 5p. Now challenge your friends to push a 10p coin through the hole without tearing the paper. In case any of your friends are a little too enthusiastic about these challenges, it is worth pointing out that hiring a chainsaw to slice the 10p piece in half is also forbidden. In fact, the trick requires no use of force whatsoever. You just fold the paper in half so that the hole is in the middle of the crease, put the 10p over the hole and lift the top corners of the paper. This has the effect of widening the hole, allowing the 10p to slip through unhindered.

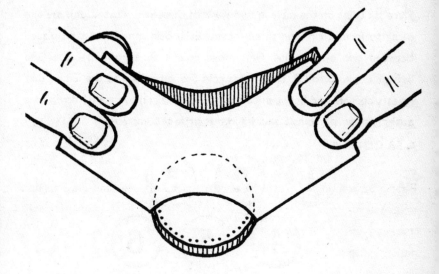

Money Ring

Skill Level: ❸

YOU WILL NEED:

SIX COINS

Place six coins on the table in two rows of three (see illustration), the aim being to form a circle in three moves. Each coin moved must be placed between two other coins. First move coin 4 to a position below and between coins 5 and 6. Then move coin 5 one position to the left so that it rests beneath and between coins 1 and 2. Finally move coin 1 down to a position between coins 5 and 4 and the circle is complete.

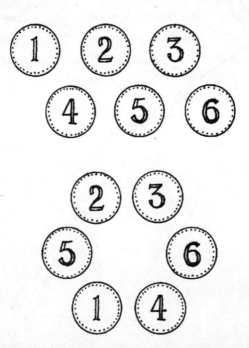

Sporting Triangles

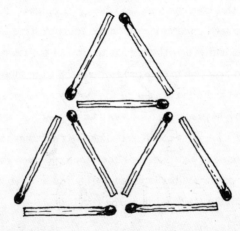 **Skill Level: ❸**

YOU WILL NEED:
NINE MATCHES

This is another ingenious puzzle with matches. Arrange nine matches in a row on the table so that they form three adjoining triangles. Now challenge anyone to make five triangles from the set-up by moving just two of the matches. All you do is take one match from each of the inside struts of the middle triangle and form a new triangle on top of the other two. You end up with four small triangles and one large one.

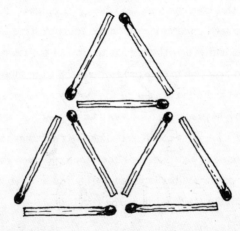

Coin Through The Table

Skill Level: ③

YOU WILL NEED:
TWO COINS, PEN AND PAPER, STICKY TAPE

Produce two coins and ask one of your group to put his initials on a tiny scrap of paper and to stick the paper on to each coin so that, in the wake of your trickery, they will be readily identifiable as the originals. Place the coins on the table, one near the edge closest to you and the other a few inches away. Pick up the farther coin in your left hand and give the impression of picking up the coin by the edge in your right hand. Instead you use your right hand to knock that coin into your lap where it is gathered by your left hand which is then placed underneath the table. Your left hand is now clenched under the table and your right hand is on top of the table. The audience believe there to be a coin in each hand whereas in truth there are two coins in your left hand and none in your right. Announce that you are now going to make the coin in your right hand work its way through the table to your left hand. After a pregnant pause, you clink the two coins together in your left hand as if one has just landed on the other and open your right fist to reveal that the coin there has vanished. Finally you bring your left hand out from underneath the table and show the two coins.

Cocktail
Shaker

 **Skill Level: ❸**

YOU WILL NEED:
A COCKTAIL MENU, PENCIL AND PAPER

Sometimes you need a break from your local. Maybe the new landlord's chosen Basil Fawlty as his role model, or they've stopped serving your favourite lager or they've painted over your graffiti in the toilets. So you seek out pastures new – perhaps that quiet little pub where they show the "Shopping Channel" instead of "Sky Sports", or the pub by the train station with its Wet Anorak competitions, or that trendy Australian theme bar where, for complete authenticity, the bar staff are all ex-cons. There will also be an extensive cocktail list with names like Kangaroo Kick, Melbourne Cup and Echidna Surprise, none of which have ever been drunk by Australians. If the cocktail list boasts 18 or more items, you can indulge in a quick prediction game based on the numbers trick. Find the 18th cocktail on the menu – let's say it's Platypus Punch – and tell your drinking partner that's the one you're going to choose and you hope he does the same. He is undecided so you suggest a simple way of making up his mind for him. Give him a pencil and paper and ask him to write down any three-figure number, as long as the digits are all different. Tell him to reverse that number and to subtract the smaller total from the larger. Lick your lips saying you can almost taste that Platypus Punch and then ask him to add up the three digits he is left with. The answer will be 18 and so you count down 18 items and order him a Platypus Punch. You knew he'd come round to your way of thinking.

Salt and Pepper

Skill Level: ❸

YOU WILL NEED:
SALT, PEPPER, A PLASTIC COMB

This trick also relies upon the ability of a plastic comb to form static electricity. Pour a little salt on to the table and sprinkle a few grains of pepper on top. Now announce that you are going to separate all the salt and pepper in just 10 seconds. Run the comb through your hair to create static electricity and pass it over the salt and pepper pile. As you do so, the grains of pepper should leap up into the teeth of the comb, leaving the salt behind on the table. But don't try using the comb on your hair again for a while unless you want the sort of dandruff which makes people sneeze.

Folding Money

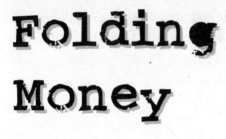 **Skill Level:** ❸

YOU WILL NEED:
A BANKNOTE

People are always impressed by tricks involving money, particularly when
it's not their money that's being used. And since the chances of getting £5
out of most of your friends are pretty remote, you might as well use your
own money for this trick. Take a £5 note (you can use any denomination,
but the lowest is safest just in case anything goes wrong) and hold it
upright so that everyone can see the Queen looking regally ahead
towards the fruit machine and the jukebox. Fold the note in half by
folding the top edge down towards you. Take the right edge and fold that
over to the left edge so that the note is now folded in quarters and then
fold it again from the right so that it is now in eighths. Next unfold the
two doubled corners from the back by taking them to the right (the note
is now back in quarters) and then open to the left the part of the note
facing you so that your £5 note is folded in half. Finally lift the front half
of the note and the Queen will be seen to be upside down. You have
somehow made her stand on her head without turning the note over.

The Secret Packet

Skill Level: ❹

YOU WILL NEED:
A COIN, A SQUARE PIECE OF PAPER, A PENCIL

Magicians love nothing more than making your money disappear and this trick presents another opportunity for them to fritter away your hard-earned cash. Place a coin on a square of paper and fold the bottom edge of the paper to within about 1cm of the top. Fold both of the sides behind the paper and finally fold that top centimetre strip back and away from you. From their viewpoint, the audience will think that the coin is safely pocketed with no visible means of escape, but your folding has created an open edge at the top. Turn the packet over so that the open edge is now at the bottom, gripping the paper so that the coin can't fall out. Tap the coin with a pencil to show everyone that it is still there. Then pass your left hand over the paper to conceal the movement of the coin, at the same time releasing your grip on the packet with your right hand and allowing the coin to fall into your palm. Keep the coin hidden there and tear up the packet amidst great pomp and ceremony. To widespread amazement (with perhaps a little apathy thrown in), the coin has vanished.

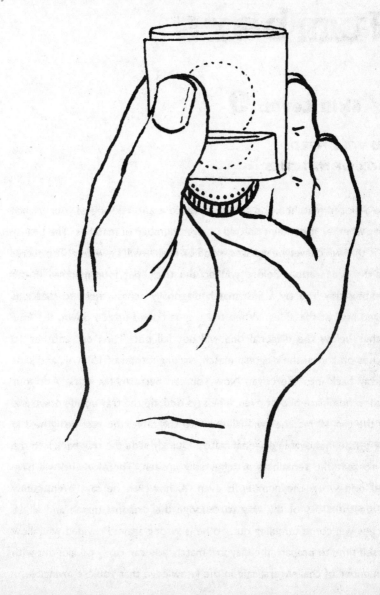

Matching Numbers

 **Skill Level: ❹**

YOU WILL NEED:
A BOX OF MATCHES

Place a closed matchbox on the table, rattle it and ask one of your friends to bet whether it contains an odd or even number of matches. The beauty of it is that whichever he guesses – odd or even – will be wrong. The secret is in the preparation. Before you do the trick, put four matches in the matchbox tray and lay a fifth match diagonally across them so that it is wedged against the sides. When the tray is tipped upside down, the four matches below the diagonal one will not fall out. Then put another 10 matches on top of the diagonal match, making a total of 15 in all, and slide the tray back into the cover. Now you can perform the trick. Ask your friend to nominate odd or even. If he says odd, tip the tray upside down and only the top 10 matches will fall out into the table, the rest being held in place by the immovable diagonal match. Quickly slide the tray back into the box so that the remaining matches stay unseen. Therefore he will have called odd when the number is even. If, however, he says even, gently squeeze the sides of the tray to dislodge the diagonal match and all 15 matches will come tumbling out. So he is wrong again. Provided you allow yourself time to prepare the diagonal match, you can carry on like this with any number of challengers, safe in the knowledge that you are invincible.

Double Your Money

Skill Level: ❹

YOU WILL NEED:
A MATCHBOX, TWO SMALL COINS

Prepare for this trick by sliding a coin under the lid at one end of a matchbox so that it is wedged in place half protruding from the box. Then gently slide the drawer of the box partly open over it, concealing the coin beneath the lid. Now you can show the half-open matchbox to your audience. You can even turn it upside down in order to convince them that the drawer is empty. Borrow from a member of the audience a coin of similar denomination to the hidden one and tell him you're going to double his money. Shut the drawer, whisper a few magic words and, when you open it again, by the powers of Houdini or by the rivers of Babylon or whatever, there are now two coins. The explanation is simple. When the drawer is shut, the wedged coin falls in. But just to be on the safe side, position a finger at the back of the matchbox in case the closing of the drawer forces the coin out. That way, you can push it back in again so that it drops safely into the drawer.

Coin Bluff

 **Skill Level:** ❹

YOU WILL NEED:
THREE SMALL COINS

Every pub has its bore – the guy who reckons he knows everything but really knows nothing. He is a mass of wild rumours, all so unlikely that even the Sunday Sport wouldn't give them much credence. Over the past few months, he has collared you at the bar with definite news – "it's gospel, I swear" – that Keith Richards is Barbara Cartland's secret love child; that Apollo 11 never went anywhere near the Moon and landed in a remote part of Mongolia by mistake; and that Lassie was really two Yorkshire terriers stitched together. Since he claims to be the fount of all knowledge, he will claim to know exactly how a magician does a particular trick even though, inevitably, he'll be hopelessly wide of the mark. There's nothing he likes more than catching someone out. So he'll be rubbing his hands with glee while you do this trick, only to discover that it has a nasty sting in the tail which might just reduce him to silence for a second or two. He sees you holding two coins flat on top of each other between your thumb and forefinger and claiming that by rubbing them together, you will produce a third coin. What he can't see is that you do have a third coin, tucked away in the palm of your hand near the base of your thumb. Anyway you rub away frantically and the speed of movement does create the impression that there are three coins. But he won't fall for that and will denounce it as just an optical illusion… whereupon you casually toss the three coins on to the table.

The Falling Pound

Skill Level: ⑤

YOU WILL NEED:
A GLASS, A 10P COIN, A MATCH, A BEER MAT

The title of this trick is a little misleading because, unless you possess a very large match – the sort which could have been used to light Apollo 11 – it is better to perform it with a lightweight 10p piece rather than a pound coin. Take a beer mat (preferably one that is dry and not sodden in ale) and place it across the top of an empty glass. The best part of the trick is making the glass empty in the first place. With the edges of the mat overlapping the rim, rest a match on the card and on top of the match, balance a 10p coin. As the tension builds to an unbearable crescendo, flick the mat forward (taking care not to send the glass flying as you do so) and the coin should drop into the glass while the match doesn't. It's all to do with the coin's inertia. Instead of a coin on a match, you can do the trick with an egg on a matchbox, but it's a lot messier. Anyway, who wants to spend most of the evening with an egg in their pocket?

The Three Glass Trick

 **Skill Level: ❺**

YOU WILL NEED:
THREE EMPTY GLASSES

Here's a nice little puzzle to play just before closing time when everyone is in the mood for intellectual stimulation and the table is stacked with empty glasses. Take three glasses and stand them in a row, turning the glasses at each end upside down. Only the glass in the middle is upright. Explain that the challenge is to turn all three the right way up in three moves. Even the old drunk who's been propping up the bar for the past five hours could just about manage that (although he might incur a few breakages en route), but you then casually add that each move must involve two glasses being turned over simultaneously. Suddenly it's not so easy, but it can be done. If everyone is struggling and the bar staff are waiting to collect the glasses, keep them in suspense no longer. The first move is to turn over one end glass and the middle glass. Then you turn over both end glasses and finally the same two glasses from the first move (end and middle). This will leave you with all three glasses standing upright, which is more than can be said for the bloke at the bar.

Clunk Clink, Every Trick

Skill Level: ⑤

YOU WILL NEED:
A COIN, A NAPKIN, A GLASS

Show your friends a coin and a napkin and then place the coin in the centre of the napkin and hold it aloft so that you are gripping the coin through the napkin. In your left hand, take a glass and cover it with the napkin. Once the glass is hidden from view, tilt it forward slightly. Now release the coin and it should clink against the side of the glass and drop into your left hand, but, on hearing the clinking sound, everyone will assume that it has fallen into the glass. Place the covered glass on the table with your right hand, keeping the coin concealed in your left hand. Finally, remove the napkin from the glass to universal disbelief that the coin has disappeared.

Fantastic Elastic

Skill Level: ⑤

YOU WILL NEED:
TWO DIFFERENT-COLOURED ELASTIC BANDS

With the palm of your left hand facing you, put a yellow elastic band over your forefinger and middle finger and a red one over your other two fingers (the colours may of course be changed according to availability). Hook the red band with the forefinger of your right hand and then do the same with the yellow band. Stretch both bands down and also put your right middle finger inside the two stretched bands. Use the two fingers to open the bands wide and then bend all four fingers on your left hand and slip them inside the two elastic bands. Quickly straighten out the fingers on your left hand, keeping them inside the bands, and the bands should change positions so that the red band is now on your left forefinger and middle finger and the yellow band is wrapped around the other two fingers.

Rapid Coin Movement

 **Skill Level: ⑤**

YOU WILL NEED:
A COIN, A RING

For this trick, you should wear a ring on your left hand – not for any show of marital solidarity, but because of the sound effect it will create. Hold a coin up for all to see and pop it into the palm of either hand. You now transfer it rapidly from one hand to the other, ultimately keeping it in your left hand while pretending to pass it back and forth. Eventually you clench your right fist in an exaggerated manner as if holding the coin. All eyes will now be focused on that hand, enabling you to let the coin slip quietly from your left hand into your lap where you can either cover it with your pullover or cross your legs so that it is tucked under your thigh. Then you slam your right hand down on the table. As you do so (and here synchronization of sound and movement is all-important), you knock the ring on your left hand against the side of the table. Everyone will immediately assume that the sound is that of the coin in your right hand hitting the table. So when you ask them which hand the coin is in, they'll nominate the right. That is when you raise your right hand and show them that there is no coin. But there will always be someone who thinks he can outsmart you and that person may well take one look at your clenched left hand, see the ring and put two and two together. "I know where the coin is," he'll announce grandly, whereupon you open your left hand to reveal a distinct absence of money. Cue egg on face. Even if your spectators are not blessed with inquisitive minds and don't ask about the ring, you will still have made the coin disappear.

Double Coin Lift

 **Skill Level: ❺**

YOU WILL NEED:
TWO COINS, A GLASS WITH A STEM

If one of your number is brave enough to drink pub wine or rich enough to drink brandy, try this trick with their glass. Balance two coins opposite each other on the rim of the glass and challenge anyone to pick both coins off the glass at exactly the same time using just the thumb and index finger of one hand. This is how you do it. You put your thumb over one coin and the index finger of the same hand over the other coin. Moving your hands in unison, you slide both coins down the sides of the glass and around the base. Then you squeeze your finger and thumb together until the two coins meet and you snatch them off the glass in one movement. Although this trick may sound simple, it does require a steady hand and therefore becomes increasingly difficult – and entertaining – the longer the evening wears on.

The Disappearing Note

Skill Level: ⑥

YOU WILL NEED:
A BANKNOTE

In the finest traditions of "Blue Peter", this is a trick you made earlier. The secret is all in the preparation. Far from prying eyes, you need to fold a banknote so that, when held in a certain way, it will look as if there are two notes. Here's how you do it. First fold the note in half vertically and towards you (A). Open out the note and fold it horizontally towards you (B). Open out the note again and make a diagonal fold away from you (C). Then, after unfolding the note, make another diagonal fold away from you, this time in the opposite direction (D). Unfold the note once more and repeat the earlier horizontal fold towards you (E). By holding the note at the sides and pushing inwards, it should now form two distinct flaps. Move one flap to the left and the other to the right and you should be left with a V-shape seemingly consisting of two separate notes. If you've made a mess of it, it will always make a nice bracelet. Assuming that you have perfected the folding process, you take the contraption down to the pub with you. At an opportune moment – just when somebody says it's your round – you produce the V-shape note from your pocket and announce that you will pay for the drinks with these two notes. You then open out the note and drop it dramatically on to the table. They will see that instead of the two notes they thought you had in your hand, there is only one. You have somehow made one of the notes disappear. Any grudging admiration will quickly evaporate when you explain that you can now only afford to buy half a round.

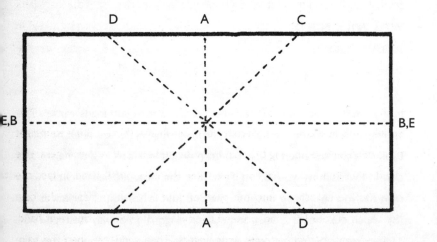

Money Go Round

Skill Level: ❻

YOU WILL NEED:
A COIN

Deception is an important feature of the magician's repertoire, making the audience's eyes deceive them. This trick, which creates the impression that a coin has travelled from one hand to the other and then vanished (whereas in truth it has been in the first hand all along), is very much part of the magician's staple diet. Hold a coin (or any other small object such as a ring or a key) in your left hand between your thumb and middle finger so that everyone can see it clearly. Announce that in your right hand you've got some priceless, magical disappearing dust which has only ever been used three times before – on Shergar, Lord Lucan and the crew of the Marie Celeste. You're going to sprinkle this dust over the coin to make it vanish into thin air. Bring your right hand down and, obscuring the coin from the audience with your fingers, give the distinct impression that you have taken the coin in that hand. In fact, the coin has merely slipped into the palm of your left hand. Keeping the coin concealed in your left hand, pretend to squeeze the coin in your right hand, seemingly manoeuvring it with your fingers. Then suddenly open the palm and fingers of your right hand to the audience to reveal that the coin has disappeared. With your right hand, search high and low for it – under beer mats, in shoes, under ashtrays – before announcing that you've spotted it. With your left hand, rummage in someone's hair and produce the coin (which, of course, has been lurking in your palm). The audience's appreciation might not run to a drink, but you may get a packet of crisps for your trouble.

Bank Roll

Skill Level: 6

YOU WILL NEED:
A BREAD ROLL, A COIN

This trick is a good surprise to play at the start of a pub meal. When the waitress comes round with her basket of bread rolls, take a roll and slip a coin into the palm of your right hand where nobody else can see it. Using your thumbs, break open the roll from underneath and then, as you push your fingers into the centre of the roll, press the coin into it. At the same time, move your thumbs up to break open the top of the roll and reveal the coin nestling within. Simply look surprised and pocket the coin whereupon everyone else will start searching inside their rolls in the hope of striking it rich. The drawback, of course, is that you shouldn't eat any roll which has had a coin inside. Oh, how we suffer for our art...

Line 'Em Up

Skill Level: ❻

YOU WILL NEED:
THREE EMPTY GLASSES, THREE FULL GLASSES

With most tricks, there is a definite purpose – a raison d'être – but the only probable result from this charade is that your beer is likely to go flat before you've had a chance to drink it. Still, here goes. Line up six pint glasses on the table, three empty and three full – although surely nobody would begrudge you that first comforting sip. The full glasses (which, for the purposes of the exercise, we will call 1, 2 and 3) should be together, followed by the empty glasses which we will call 4, 5 and 6. Thus the opening line-up is 1, 2, 3, 4, 5, 6. The aim is to swap the glasses around so that full and empty pints are positioned alternately, but you have only three moves and each move must involve moving two glasses and these must be adjacent to one another. It's a tricky one, but here's how it's done. Move full glasses 1 and 2 to the other end of the line so that the order is now 3, 4, 5, 6, 1, 2. Next move empty glass 6 and full glass 1 to the far right of the line, making the order 3, 4, 5, 2, 6, 1. Finally switch full glass 3 and empty glass 4 to a position between empty glass 5 and full glass 2. So you end up with an order of 5, 3, 4, 2, 6, 1 – empty, full, empty, full, empty, full. Now that's over, you can get on with your pint.

A Financial Riddle

Skill Level: ⑥

YOU WILL NEED:
TWO 2P COINS, ONE 1P COIN

You need to be at your most alert to solve this problem – a mind befuddled by alcohol will struggle all the way through happy hour. Place a 1p coin on the table and then put a 2p piece on either side so that both of the higher-denomination coins are touching the 1p. The challenge is to move one of the 2p coins to a position between the 1p and the other 2p whilst adhering to three strict rules – the 2p on the left must not be touched; the 1p can be touched, but must not be moved; and the 2p on the right, being an exceedingly emotional coin, may be touched and moved. After the sum of intellects present have proved hopelessly unequal to the task, you can step in and show them how to do it. You put a finger from your left hand on the 1p and a finger from your right hand on the 2p on the right. With your finger, you move the 2p a little to the right and then bring it back and knock it against the 1p. Since the 1p and the 2p on the left are touching, this move creates a knock-on effect, forcing the 2p further to the left and creating a gap between it and the 1p. As you are allowed to move the 2p on the right, you can now swing it round into the space between the other two coins. Cue everyone else muttering: "I wish I'd thought of that…"

10 Match Lift

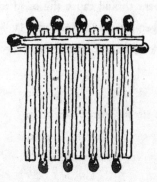 **Skill Level:** ⑥

YOU WILL NEED:
ELEVEN MATCHES

The challenge here is to use a solitary match to pick up another 10. To do so, you need to arrange the matches carefully on the table. Lay one match horizontally and nine more vertically across it, alternate matches facing in opposite directions. In other words, the heads of the odd-numbered matches will face one way and the even-numbered matches will face the other way. Finally place another match horizontally on top of the arrangement so that it is directly above the very first match to have been laid, but pointing in the opposite direction. Using the thumb and forefinger of both hands, you now firmly grip the ends of the two parallel matches and the matches sandwiched in between will also be raised from the table. Thus you have accomplished your mission of using one match to lift the other 10.

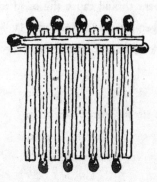

The Jumping Band

 **Skill Level:** ❼

YOU WILL NEED:
AN ELASTIC BAND

It sounds impossible – the stuff of which dreams are made – but, with practice, you can make an elastic band jump from one finger to another. Loop an elastic band around the forefinger of your left hand and, with your right hand, stretch it across so that it passes behind the middle finger of your left hand. Then, taking care not to twist the band, pull it back down around your middle finger so that it loops on to your forefinger again. Pause for a second and announce that you are now going to make the elastic band leap from your forefinger to the middle finger. Bend your middle finger slightly and the movement should cause the band to jump the divide and land on your middle finger. However, more than likely it will end up on the floor… in which case try again. Remember, nobody goes home until you get it right.

Roll With It

🦉 **Skill Level: ❼**

YOU WILL NEED:
A BREAD ROLL, A FORK, A NAPKIN

If you take the precaution of saving a bread roll, here's another stunt you can perform at the end of a pub meal. While the others are wrestling over custody of the one after-dinner mint, quietly stick the prongs of your fork into the roll at an angle and slip the roll and its new handle on your lap under your napkin. When the fuss has died down, say you're going to make your roll walk the tightrope. Taking a corner between the first two fingers of each hand, hold the napkin aloft so that it forms a small screen between you and the others and at the same time pick up the handle of the fork between your right thumb and forefinger. Keep the fork hidden behind the napkin and position it so that the roll appears balanced on top of the napkin. By moving the fork, you can make it look as though the roll is walking along the edge of the napkin.

The Great Escape

Skill Level: ❼

YOU WILL NEED:
A GLASS, A BEER MAT, A COIN, A PIECE OF PAPER

Declare your intention of making an ordinary coin burrow its way through a beer mat into a glass below. Follow the procedure in "The Secret Packet" by putting a coin on a square of paper and folding the paper so that you leave an unseen gap at the top. When you turn the packet upside down, the coin slides out into your hand. Place an empty glass on the table and pick up a beer mat between the thumb and forefinger of your right hand, keeping the coin hidden in the same hand. Rest the mat over the mouth of the glass, at the same time using your thumb to force the coin forward and to wedge it between the mat and the rim of the glass where nobody can see it. Now set the paper packet, which everyone thinks contains the coin, on top of the mat. Open your hand to show that it is empty and tap the beer mat. The vibration will cause the coin to drop into the glass and your stunned audience will think that it has somehow worked its way out of the packet and penetrated the beer mat.

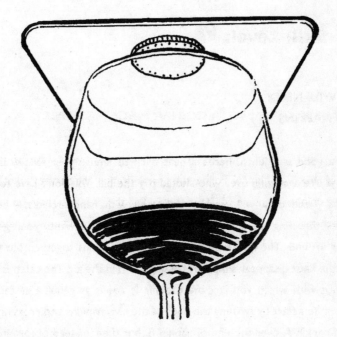

Flying Napkins

 **Skill Level: ❼**

YOU WILL NEED:
TWO NAPKINS

After a good pub lunch, here's a neat trick to amuse your fellow diners while you're agonizing over who should pay the bill. You don't have to use napkins – the trick will work equally well with handkerchiefs – but it involves throwing them in the air and not everyone wants your germs wafting around. The idea is that you knot two napkins together, but then make the knot disappear simply by tossing them in the air. The catch is that the knot with which you link the napkins is about as genuine as canned laughter. You start by twisting the ends of the two napkins and crossing the end of napkin A over the end of napkin B, but then, instead of forming an ordinary knot, you cross the end of napkin B around the end of napkin A above the lower part of napkin B. Pass the end of napkin B over and across the end of napkin A, bringing down the end of napkin A over napkin B and through the loop which has been created. Tighten it and everyone will think you've tied a perfectly ordinary knot. Holding aloft the free end of napkin A, show everyone the two napkins seemingly tied together then suddenly hurl them into the air and they will fall separately to the floor.

What a Corker!

Skill Level: ❼

YOU WILL NEED:
AN EMPTY WINE BOTTLE, A CORK, A DRINKING STRAW

As we have discovered, even if you desert the pub for a wine bar, your scope for trickery is by no means diminished. First you need to relieve the wine bottle of its contents (there will be no shortage of volunteers willing to undertake this task) and then ask the bar staff whether they would be so kind as to furnish you with a drinking straw and a cork which is slightly too small for the bottle you have. The cork must be large enough to rest in the neck of its own accord. You then announce the aim of the trick – to blow the cork into the bottle. It may seem a fairly pointless exercise, but it's surprising what people will do after they've guzzled a bottle of wine. The natural tendency will be to blow as fiercely as possible, creating the sort of gust which brings havoc to Florida from time to time, but they will soon discover that blowing hard simply makes the cork pop out of the bottle. When everyone is breathless, produce your drinking straw and show them how it's done. For if you place the straw against the centre of the cork and blow steadily, the cork will drop into the bottle.

Fork Bending

 **Skill Level: ❼**

YOU WILL NEED:
A TABLE FORK

Uri Geller's ability to bend all manner of cutlery has made him the bane of waiters everywhere. And with this stunt you can convince your friends that you too are blessed with the powers of Mr Geller. Hold the fork upright in both fists, left hand at the top and right hand at the bottom, just above the prongs which are pointing towards the audience. Press down the fork on to the table. Your actions should suggest that you are exerting great force, a feeling which could be communicated by shaking hands, the odd grimace and a bead or two of sweat. As you press down, allow the handle to fall back through your fingers so that it assumes a position approximately parallel to the table. Your fists and wrists obscure the dropping handle which is held in place solely by the little finger of the right hand, but, from the audience's head-on view, it will appear that you have bent the fork at right angles. When everybody looks suitably amazed, release your two-handed grip and show them that the fork hasn't bent one degree, let alone 90. They might not be too thrilled by your deception, but at least the waiter will be relieved.

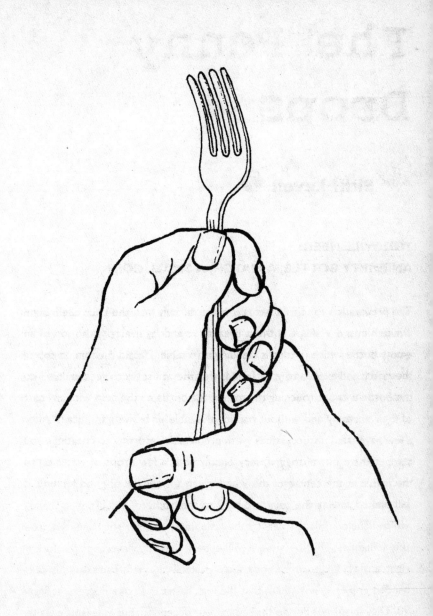

The Penny Drops

 Skill Level: **7**

YOU WILL NEED:
AN EMPTY BOTTLE, A MATCH, A SMALL COIN

The preparation for this is actually more difficult than the trick itself. Bend a match into a V shape without breaking it and lay it across the top of an empty bottle which in turn is standing on a table. Place a 1p coin on top of the match and explain to your friends that they must try to get the coin into the bottle without touching the match, the bottle or the coin with any part of their anatomy and without rocking the table or blowing frantically. After a few have tried unsuccessfully (with predictable resorting to cheating), you can put them out of their misery. Simply pour a few drops of water on to the match at the centre of the V and, given a modicum of good fortune, it will open, allowing the coin to drop into the bottle.

Water, Water Everywhere

 **Skill Level: ❼**

YOU WILL NEED:
TWO IDENTICAL LONG-STEM WINE GLASSES

You should only attempt this trick if you are on extremely friendly terms with the landlord. Otherwise the sight of you balancing one of his precious wine glasses in your mouth might encourage him to order the rottweiler that passes as a doorman to feel your collar and eject you into the night air. In truth, this is more of a stunt than a trick. To set it up, you need two long-stemmed wine glasses, the sort in which the landlord serves his warm Chardonnay. Partly fill one glass with water. You can use any liquid but, in the likely event of spillage, the loss of water is less traumatic, not to mention cheaper, than scotch. Stand this glass on the table and then balance another identical glass, this time empty, upside down on top of it so that the two glasses are rim to rim. The challenge is to pour the contents of the lower glass into the upper glass without anyone touching the upper glass with their hands and without setting the upper glass on a firm surface (floor, table or chair) until the contents of the lower glass have been transferred into it. The way to do it is to bend over, pick up the base of the upper glass with your mouth and, standing up, to tilt your head back slightly so that the glass is upright and the bowl of the glass is kept in position by your nose. Your hands are still free so you are able to pick up the other glass and pour the contents into the glass held between your teeth. It's not a pretty sight and is probably not something to perform on a first date, unless you want it to be your last.

Sticky Dice

Skill Level: 7

YOU WILL NEED:
THREE DICE

Put the three dice down on a table and ask one of your fellow revellers to pick them up between tip of thumb and forefinger. Then tell him or her to drop the middle dice while still keeping hold of the dice on either side. It sounds easy, but it's not and attempts will invariably end in failure – until, of course, you show how it's done. Before your turn, sneakily lick your finger and thumb (this can be done under the pretence of removing a lump of pork scratching from your teeth). The moisture provides extra adhesion to your digits when you press them firmly on to the sides of the dice. Open your finger and thumb quickly, let the middle dice slip out and close them again immediately. You may wish to practise this trick for hours on end in the privacy of your own home, but only if you're a particularly sad individual.

Candle in the Wind

 **Skill Level:** **7**

YOU WILL NEED:
A CANDLE, A BOTTLE

Unless you frequent a pub which has candles on the table, this trick is more suited to a wine bar. You position a sizeable bottle between yourself and the candle, press your face up to the bottle and blow against the surface. With any luck the candle should go out as if you have blown right through the bottle. The explanation is that when you blow on the surface of the bottle, your breath divides into two air currents which travel around the bottle and join up again on the other side to extinguish the candle. The really ambitious performer may care to try this trick with two or three bottles lined up between himself and the candle.

Matchsticks

 **Skill Level:** **7**

YOU WILL NEED:
A BOOK OF MATCHES

To set up this trick, take a book of matches and bend one match away from its original position, strike its head and blow out the flame. Place the book of matches inside your jacket pocket and head for the pub. When the conversation starts to flag, tell everyone that you are about to amaze them with a feat of magic. With your right hand, remove the book of matches from your pocket, holding the base between the finger and thumb so that the spent match, which is still attached to the book, is concealed by your thumb. Show the contents to your audience so that they can see all of the matches in the book are live. Now with your left hand, remove one of the live matches and strike it against the book. Close the book from front to back, pivoting the bent match so that it is now inside the book. Secure the cover and wave the lighted match around the book. Then pull back the cover to reveal that one match magically appears spent. While everyone tries to work out how it was done, say you'll put them out of their misery if somebody will refill your glass.

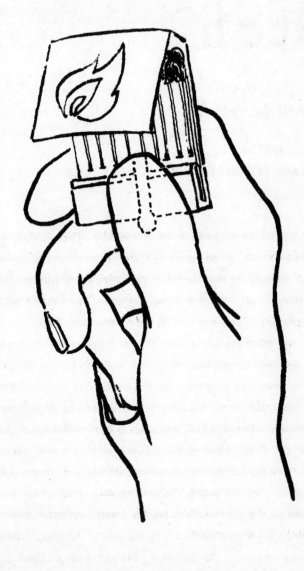

The Big Match

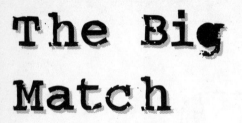

 **Skill Level: 8**

YOU WILL NEED:
TWO GLASS TUMBLERS, FIVE LARGE MATCHES

Place two glass tumblers upside down on the table. They don't have to be identical, but should be smooth-sided. Put three matches under one tumbler and carefully set the fourth match in a horizontal position between the two glasses, about a quarter of the way down. The head of this match should be pressed against the side of the tumbler which has no matches beneath it. Bet someone a pint that you can remove the three matches under the glass without allowing the match which forms the bridge to fall to the table. Since the solution is by no means obvious, he will almost certainly accept. But there's still a fair bit of work to be done before you can taste that pint. To bring it off, you need to ignite a fifth match and hold that against the head of the wedged match so that it too ignites. The moment the wedged match bursts into flame, blow it out – not too fiercely or you may dislodge the match. Then allow it to cool down for a few moments and lift the glass which its head is pressed against. All being well, the head of the dead match will stick to the side of the glass, enabling you to remove the matches under the other glass and claim your pint. The key to success is the length of time you leave the match to cool – if you are too hasty, it won't stick to the glass and you'll stay thirsty.

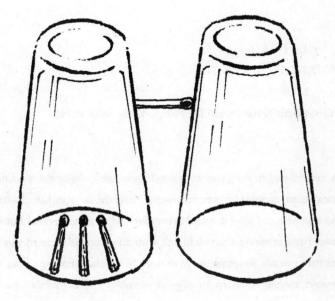

Snap!

Skill Level: ❽

YOU WILL NEED:
A BANKNOTE, A PENCIL

Warning: This trick could be dangerous. Take care!

There are no end of things which sound impossible – winning the Olympic 100 metres on a Spacehopper, hearing an original song in the charts, and getting a half-decent meal at a motorway service station, to name but three. You could add breaking a pencil in half with a five-pound note to this list… except that you are about to prove that it can be done. Fold the note in half lengthways, making as sharp an edge as possible. This is merely a harmless diversion, but will help convince spectators that the note does possess a cutting edge. Grip the note firmly at one end between thumb and forefinger (keeping the latter behind the note, out of sight) and ask someone to hold an ordinary pencil in a horizontal position. The pencil should also be held tightly. Bring the sharpened edge of the note swiftly down on to the pencil, extending your forefinger at the moment of impact. The pencil should snap in two, but as a result of the blow from your finger rather than from the banknote. Immediately the pencil has broken, withdraw your forefinger and nobody will suspect any subterfuge… unless a large bruise suddenly appears on your finger.

The Jamaica Bottle Stunt

 **Skill Level:** ⑧

YOU WILL NEED:
A LONG-NECKED BOTTLE

Warning: This trick could be dangerous. Take care!

If you're about as good a limbo dancer as Bernard Manning, you are advised to give this one a miss because it requires a great deal of athleticism. It is definitely not for someone whose idea of physical exertion is a game of chess or who has to have a lie down after reading the Sporting Life. The equipment consists of a long-necked bottle placed upright on the floor. Then, with your left hand holding your right ear, your right arm behind your back and your right hand holding your left foot, you have to bend down and pick up the top of the bottle in your mouth before straightening up again without losing either bottle or balance and without releasing your grip on your right ear or left foot. Phew!

Raising the Money

 **Skill Level:** ⑧

YOU WILL NEED:
FIVE STRAWS, A 5P COIN

If you have the misfortune to find yourself in one of those large, modern featureless chain pubs which serve identical meals and not only welcome families, but virtually refuse to serve you unless you've got children with you (it would be no surprise to see a sign: OVER-18s WILL ONLY BE SERVED WITH ALCOHOL IF ACCOMPANIED BY SOMEONE UNDER 10), you can at least pass the time with a trick or two involving drinking straws. For the one thing you can be certain of at such establishments is that there will be no shortage of free fun packs, badges and straws. So, after you've suffered the indignity of ordering Percy the Puffin's Kiddies Special, pluck five straws from a container and a 5p coin from your pocket and challenge anyone to lift four straws and the coin, using just one other straw. The secret is to build a solid construction. Place the first two straws in an X-shape on the table and put the coin on top of them where they meet in the middle. Put another straw vertically down either side of the X so that these two straws pass over and under the existing straws, but at opposite ends.

Finally thread the fifth straw through the centre of the contraption horizontally so that it supports the other straws and the coin. Raise the horizontal straw gently and the whole thing should lift off the table. It does require a degree of dexterity so it's best not to ask the poor waitress whose turn it is to play Percy the Puffin to participate, especially if she's still wearing her flippers.

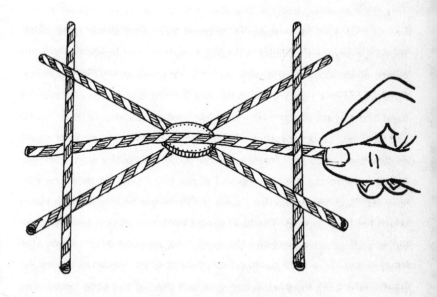

The Snapping Band

 **Skill Level:** ❾

YOU WILL NEED:
A LONG ELASTIC BAND

This trick also requires considerable manual skill as you convince your friends that you have magically restored a broken elastic band. After showing everyone that there is nothing hidden in your hands, you grip the centre of the double band with your left hand and insert the thumb and forefinger of your right hand into the loop formed at either end. Stretch the band into a figure of eight with your left hand and move your right thumb and forefinger closer together, allowing the loop which was on your thumb to slide over on to your forefinger. Now put the remaining fingers on your right hand into the double loop and at the other side, do the same with your left hand, using your left thumb and forefinger to grip the loose knot which has been formed. The band should be stretched taut between your hands and, although double, should give the appearance of being single. Then remove your right forefinger from the loop and move the thumb and forefinger of both hands close together, still gripping the band tightly in its double loop. Pull your hands sharply apart and the band will make a snapping sound. As your hands separate to reveal the two ends of the double band, everyone will be convinced that it has broken. Ease your fingers from the band, enabling it to return to its single state, and cup it in both hands. Get someone to tap on your cupped hands with a pencil, beer mat or whatever happens to be around, and open them up to reveal a perfectly sound elastic band.

The Sliding Thumb

Skill Level: ⑨

There are several ways of removing the tip of your left thumb – such as inspecting an alligator's teeth for signs of plaque – but by far the most painless is this nimble trick much loved by pub illusionists down the years. To make it look convincing requires a great deal of practice. Start with your left hand in front of you, Napoleon-like, so that the palm faces your body and the fingers and thumb are all in a line pointing to your right. Cover the first knuckle of your left thumb with your right forefinger, bend the top part of your left thumb downwards and position your right thumb in such a way that its tip appears to replace that of the left thumb. Obviously this should be done as quickly and smoothly as possible, which is where all those hours of practice in front of a mirror come in. Keeping the thumbs in place, clench the remaining fingers of your right hand so that the audience can get a good view of what is about to happen. Finally hold your left hand still and slide your right thumb along the top of your left forefinger. You can then complete the return journey to a mixture of wonderment and horror, depending on how squeamish your friends are.

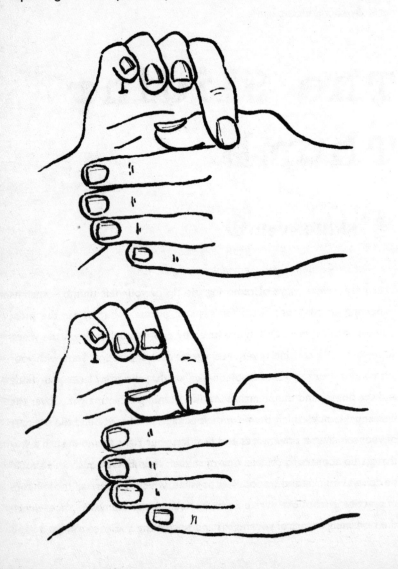

Water to Wine

Skill Level: 10

YOU WILL NEED:
TWO WINE GLASSES, RED WINE, WATER, A PIECE OF
THICK PAPER OR VERY THIN CARDBOARD

P.S. Given the difficulty of this trick, it is advisable to practise with cheap plonk rather than best Beaujolais.

Tell your friends that you are going to perform a trick that has only ever been done once before... and that was nearly 2000 years ago, by Jesus Christ. You are going to convert water into wine and, somewhat less attractively, vice-versa. First inform everyone of the masterplan. You will be taking two identical wine glasses, one filled to the brim with water, the other filled to the brim with red wine, and then you will put the two glasses together in such a way that the wine and the water will change places of their own accord. At this juncture, should anyone be foolish enough to bet you that it can't be done, bite their hand off... as long as you are confident of your expertise. The trick goes like this. First cover the glass of water with a piece of thick paper or very thin cardboard. A beer mat may prove too thick. The piece should be large enough to cover the glass with half an inch all round to spare. Holding the paper against the glass with the palm of your hand, quickly turn the glass upside down. You can now release your hand from the paper which should cling to the rim of the glass, preventing spillage. Without removing the paper from the inverted glass, place that glass on top of the wine-filled glass in such a manner that the rim of the upper glass lines up precisely with the rim of the lower glass. With a steady hand (so perform this trick before you've drunk too much) slightly withdraw the paper from between the two glasses until there is a small space of not more than a quarter of an inch in width between the edge of the paper and the rims of the glasses. To the astonishment of your audience, the water will slowly descend through the opening you made by withdrawing the paper partition and will force the wine to rise through the same opening into the upper glass. This process will continue until all of the water has settled in the lower glass, previously occupied by the wine, and all of the wine has moved into the upper glass formerly occupied by the water. The problem of how to separate the two glasses after the trick has been completed without drenching everyone with water and wine should be for someone else to solve. You've earned a drink!

Raise a Glass

Skill Level: ⑩

YOU WILL NEED:
TWO IDENTICAL GLASSES, A SMALL CANDLE, A PIECE OF PAPER

It's almost chucking out time. The bell has gone for last orders, the karaoke machine has been put away so you don't have to endure any more versions of "White Christmas" sung by old Uncle Roy, and over in the corner a young man appears spell-bound by his girlfriend's eyes until you realize he is about to throw up over her top. But if you're in a pub or wine bar which has candles on the table, there is still one last trick you can perform before heading home. Put an empty glass tumbler on the table and challenge anyone to lift it off the table by magnetizing it with another tumbler. It's pretty difficult so, if you don't want to end up with a hefty bill for breakages, show them how it's done. Take a small piece of burning candle and place it in the bottom of the glass so that the flame doesn't extend beyond the rim. Then cover the glass with a piece of soggy paper and invert the second glass on top of the paper so that the rims of the two glasses are lined up precisely. As you lift the upper tumbler, the lower one should also rise from the table as if magnetized. If it doesn't work, you can always find another local, preferably one which doesn't have karaoke nights.

Chapter Four:

Tricks With Everyday Objects

Nailed On

⚰ Skill Level: ❶

YOU WILL NEED:
A BOX OF COLOURED WAX CRAYONS

Sometimes a magician has to work overtime to make a trick appear convincing and only the brilliance of your patter will make this one seem anything other than a total con. The premise is promising enough – without looking, you are able to determine the colour of a chosen crayon – but the reality is mind-numbingly simple. You begin by putting a box of wax crayons on the table and, while your back is turned, ask someone to take one crayon from the box. Order the other crayons to be taken away and ask for the chosen one to be handed to you behind your back. At this stage, there is no way that you can have seen which crayon has been selected. Now for the chicanery. With the crayon behind your back, pretend that you are feeling it for inspiration (what rubbish magicians talk!), but instead dig the thumb nail of your right hand into the wax. Keeping the crayon out of sight behind your back, bring your right arm out in front of you and gesture to the person that he must really concentrate hard on the colour so that his thoughts can be transferred to you. With your arm before you, glance down at your thumb nail and the colour embedded there will be the colour of the crayon. As you put your hand back behind your back, craftily flick off the wax and name the colour. The only way this trick can fail is if you confidently shout "red" before realizing you've got a blister on your thumb.

Very Dicey

 **Skill Level:** ❶

YOU WILL NEED:
THREE DICE, PENCIL AND PAPER

Here is another opportunity to demonstrate your remarkable X-ray vision. Hand one of your friends three dice, a pencil and a piece of paper. Turn your back on him, and ask him to stack the dice in a pile and to add up the numbers on the five hidden faces (i.e., the bottom face of the top dice and the tops and bottoms of the other two dice). Tell him to write the total on the piece of paper and to put it in his pocket. You then turn around and, after nothing more than a quick glance at the dice, you are able to announce the figure on the piece of paper. It's easy really. The opposite faces of a dice always add up to seven and so the opposite faces of three dice add up to 21. All you need to do is look at the number on the upper face of the top dice and subtract it from 21. So if the top face shows six, the five hidden faces must total 15. If you need to remove shoes and socks to do this quick calculation, perhaps you should try a trick which doesn't involve any maths.

Synchronized Matches

Skill Level: ❷

YOU WILL NEED:
A BOWL OF WATER, MATCHES, A LUMP OF SUGAR, A
SMALL PIECE OF SOAP

Fortunately for the sake of our taste buds and our hygiene, most of us are able to tell the difference between a lump of sugar and a bar of soap. But if you do wake up one morning and suddenly realize that you are no longer able to differentiate between the two objects, here is a simple experiment to help you get through the day without foaming at the mouth every time you have a cup of coffee. Fill a bowl with clean water and carefully arrange a dozen or so matches in a circle on the surface so that it looks a bit like a clock face. For artistic reasons, the matches should be spaced apart equidistantly and should leave a clear circle of water in the centre. Now dip a lump of sugar into the centre circle and the matches should immediately move towards the sugar. Remove the sugar and replace it with a small piece of soap and the matches will instantly retreat back towards their original positions, the effect resembling a low-budget version of a Busby Berkeley musical. The reason for the erratic behaviour of the matches owes more to

"Tomorrow's World" than Hollywood. When you put the sugar lump in the bowl, it absorbs some of the water and a small current of water flows towards the sugar, pulling the matches with it. The soap, on the other hand, weakens the surface tension in its immediate vicinity, allowing the stronger surface tension near the edges of the bowl to drag the matches outwards. So now you know.

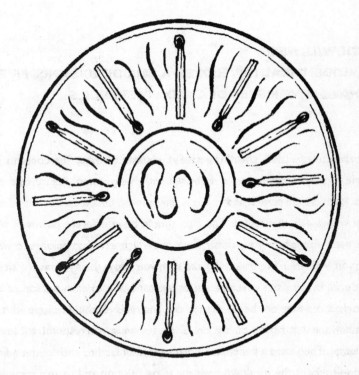

Make Your Mark

 **Skill Level: ❷**

YOU WILL NEED:
FIVE IDENTICAL ENVELOPES, A PAIR OF SCISSORS, FIVE
CHAIRS, FIVE PIECES OF CARD, FIVE PENCILS

By sheer magic (well, cheating actually), you can decipher the contents of a series of sealed envelopes as if blessed with X-ray vision. Beforehand, take five identical envelopes and make a tiny, almost undetectable, cut in each flap with a pair of scissors. The cuts should be in different positions along the flap – this is how you craftily work out which envelope belongs to which person. Ask your five friends (make sure you know their names) to sit in a line and, keeping the envelopes in order, hand one to each person so that whoever is sitting on the far right of the line receives the envelope with the cut on the far right and so on. Each cut must correspond to seating position. Then hand a pencil and a blank piece of card to each of the quintet and ask them to write down their name on the card and to seal it securely in their envelope. Ask someone to collect the envelopes and give them a good shuffle before handing them back to you. Of course, you can determine the owner of each envelope simply by looking at the cut and matching it to the chair position but, as with all the best tricks, you have to make it look much more difficult than it really is. Try gazing forlornly at the back of the envelope, praying for inspiration. You can even press the envelope to your forehead to imply that you are receiving extra-sensory messages. Finally call out a name and tear open the envelope to show that you have got it right. By the time you have done all five (although the last one is somewhat academic), there won't be a closed mouth in the house.

Get Knotted!

 **Skill Level: ❷**

YOU WILL NEED:
AN EMPTY MATCHBOX, A LENGTH OF STRING

Take a piece of string and tie it in a single knot around a matchbox, the tray of which has been removed. You then push one end of the string back through the matchbox and also push the knot off the end of the box and into the empty cover. Hold the two ends of the string, pull it taut and the knot will magically disappear. This one requires a bit of practice because you must insert the string carefully and make sure the knot slides off the side of the box. It may not earn you your own TV series, but it's mildly impressive.

Ashes to Ashes

🦉 **Skill Level: ❷**

YOU WILL NEED:
SLIPS OF PAPER, A PENCIL, A BOWL, AN ASHTRAY, A BOX OF MATCHES OR A LIGHTER

This is a good trick to play when you've got a crowd of people – seven or eight at the very least. You get everyone present to call out the name of a football team and, as they do so, you appear to write each name on a separate slip of paper which you then fold over and put into a bowl or some other vessel. Next you ask one person to choose and take one of the slips without looking at it. Now you put the remaining slips into an ashtray and set fire to them (keep the soda syphon nearby in case the blaze gets out of hand). When all are burnt to a cinder, you study the ashes carefully for a minute or so before calling out the name of the team on the missing slip. The person unfolds the slip in his or her possession and shows it to everyone else to confirm that you have made the correct deduction. Far from being able to read ashes, your only power is that of deception. Instead of writing down all of the different team names on slips of paper, you simply wrote the same name on every piece. So you couldn't fail to get it right.

Guess Who?

Skill Level: ❷

This trick once more calls upon the services of a trusty assistant – a Robin to your Batman, a Laurel to your Hardy, a Renée to your Renata. While you are out of the room, the others choose one of their number to be identified on your return. And your boast is that you will be able to name that person. You enter the room again to be confronted with a sea of faces and no obvious clues, but, unbeknown to everyone else, one of those present is a mole whose task it is to pass on a hidden message. The clue is transmitted by the secret collaborator's stance – it will be exactly the same as that of the mystery person. Clearly if everybody speaks the same body language, you could be in trouble so you may have to wait until the chosen person makes a movement which can be mimicked by your assistant. Besides, you don't want to get it right too quickly, otherwise they will all know that it's just a trick.

Sinking Sugar

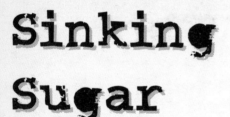 **Skill Level:** ❷

YOU WILL NEED:
FOUR SUGAR LUMPS,
A CUP OF TEA OR COFFEE

Stand three sugar lumps one on top of another in an empty cup. Carefully pour in sufficient lukewarm tea or coffee so that the top lump is just covered and the column remains undisturbed. If the beverage is too hot, the sugar will dissolve instantly and the column will crumble. Gather your friends around and tell them that you are going to make a lump of sugar float on the surface of your drink. Place it on top of the concealed pile of sugar lumps and there it will sit. With practice, you will even be able to command it to sink on cue as you correctly judge when the three supporting lumps do eventually dissolve.

Directory
Enquiries

 **Skill Level: ❸**

YOU WILL NEED:
A TELEPHONE DIRECTORY,
PENCIL AND PAPER

Only the most ardent trainspotter would dream of learning the telephone directory by heart, but after this trick your friends will be fully expecting to see you in bobble hat, tank top and anorak and armed with a copy of "The History of Steam". In front of a captivated audience, take two minutes to flick through the local phone book and at the end declare that you have memorized the entire directory and are willing to be tested on it. In fact, you have only memorized one entry – the 10th name down in the left-hand column on page 89. Ask for a volunteer to test you, first confirming that no previous dialogue has passed between the two of you as to the contents of the directory. Say that he is going to do a simple sum to pick an entry at random. Hand him a pencil and paper and tell him to write down any three numbers. Ask him to reverse them and to subtract the smaller number from the larger one. If the answer to this is less than 100, tell him to add a zero to the front (such as 099). Next get him to reverse the new number and to add it to the previous number. As you know only too well, the answer will always be 1089. For example:

$$764$$
$$-\ 467$$
$$=\ 297$$
$$+\ 792$$
$$=\ 1089$$

$$322$$
$$-\ 223$$

$$=\ 099$$

$$+\ 990$$

$$=\ 1089$$

Tell him that the first two numbers in his answer refer to the number of entries down in the first column in a particular page and that the second two refer to the actual page number. Accordingly, he turns to page 89 and counts down 10 names in the first column. After a moment's meditation, you correctly state the name and address of that entry. Everyone will be mightily impressed... but hopefully not so impressed that they want to test you further.

The Amazing Sugar Lump

 **Skill Level: ❸**

YOU WILL NEED:
A SUGAR LUMP, A SOFT PENCIL, A GLASS OF WATER

Give one of your friends a soft pencil and ask him to write a number on a cube of sugar. Have the lump (the sugar not your friend) placed on a table with the number-side down so that you can't see what it is. Meanwhile pour some water into a glass, in the process dampening your right thumb. Pick up the sugar lump, still number side down, with your right forefinger at the top and your right thumb at the bottom. Press your moistened thumb firmly against the numbered base of the cube and the number should transfer on to your flesh. Drop the sugar into the glass number side down so that you still can't see it and, as it dissolves, ask your friend to reveal the number he wrote. Hold up your thumb to show the same number.

Sixth Sense

Skill Level: ❸

YOU WILL NEED:
SIX EVERYDAY OBJECTS

This trick relies solely upon the art of deception and requires the services of an assistant. Arrange six everyday objects in a row on the table – say a comb, a pair of scissors, the remote control (if you can bear to be parted from it), a knife, a corkscrew and a potato peeler. As you are positioning them, announce which number refers to which object so that your assistant can make a mental note of each one. You then ask everybody present to concentrate really hard on one single object without telling you which one it is. In fact, so that you are unable to overhear their deliberations, you leave the room. On your return, all you need do is glance at your assistant who just happens to be leaning on the table. The number of fingers he has extended denotes the number of the chosen object. If his fist is clenched, the selected object is number six. You don't exactly have to be the Brain of Britain to work out the answer, although you could make life difficult for yourself by picking an assistant who recently lost three fingers in a bacon slicer.

Hidden Cash

 **Skill Level: ❸**

YOU WILL NEED:
AN ENVELOPE, TWO IDENTICAL SHEETS OF PAPER,
GLUE, A COIN

Stick two identical sheets of paper together so that, to the naked eye, they look like one. If any edges are overlapping, trim them away. Fold each sheet an inch up from the bottom all the way along to create a flap. Leave the front flap empty, but slip a pound coin into the back flap before putting the paper into a suitable-sized envelope. Begin the trick by removing the paper from the envelope, taking care to show only the front side to the audience. Show them the inside of the envelope to convince them that nothing is lurking within and tip it upside down so that they know beyond doubt that the envelope is empty. Similarly, unfold the flap on the front side of the paper so that they can see that nothing is hidden. Fold the flap up again and replace the paper in the envelope. Now announce that by the miracles of modern science, you are going to conjure up a one pound coin. Take the paper from the envelope, this time showing only the back sheet to the audience, and open the flap to reveal the coin.

Skin Deep

Skill Level: ❸

YOU WILL NEED:

AN ORANGE, AN APPLE, A SHARP KNIFE, A LARGE HANDKERCHIEF

Some people can remember clearly what they were doing on the day Kennedy was assassinated – and, given that still nobody seems to know who was responsible, it's quite handy to have an alibi. Others are able to recall their precise whereabouts on the day England won the 1966 World Cup, or when Take That split up, or on the day when no furniture shop had a sale. Well, this trick is so awe-inspiring that it will have those who were privileged enough to witness it talking about it in the same breath as those other great historical events. They will proudly recall being there on the day you changed an orange into an apple! To make this stunning illusion work, you first need to use a sharp knife to peel the skin from an orange into four quarters. The orange must be peeled so that the skin remains joined at the top and when placed carefully on a table still looks intact from a distance. Take your orange and place it around an apple. Seeing it for the first time, your audience will think it is a perfectly ordinary orange because they won't be close enough to spot any cuts in the skin. Drape a large handkerchief over the orange and say that you'd rather have an apple. Grip the orange skin through the handkerchief, pull it away and slip the crumpled up handkerchief containing the orange skin into your pocket. All that is left on the table is the apple.

Sugar Toss

Skill Level: ❸

YOU WILL NEED:
TWO LUMPS OF SUGAR, AN EMPTY WHISKY GLASS

Ask one of your friends to hold an empty whisky glass in his hand with a lump of sugar wedged between his thumb and the side of the glass. Thumb and sugar should be approximately half-way down the side of the glass. Balance a second lump on top of the first one and bet him that, without using his other hand, he can't toss each lump into the glass, one at a time. It sounds easy enough and indeed it is at first, but it's the second lump which proves the downfall of so many. For, having tossed the first lump safely into the shallow glass, they find that it leaps out again when they try to repeat the feat with the second lump. After all of your friends have tried and failed, show them how the professionals do it. Toss the first lump into the air and catch it in the glass, but instead of tossing the second lump high, simply perform a minimal upward movement, release your thumb, allowing the sugar to fall, and bring the glass down to pouch the plummeting lump. Some may call it cheating and you can agree with them... over the drinks they've had to buy you.

The Suspended Egg

 Skill Level: ❸

YOU WILL NEED:
AN EGG, A JUG OF WATER, SALT

If you put an egg into a jug of water, it will sink to the bottom because it is denser than water, but if you add a quantity of salt to the water, stirring it until it dissolves, the egg will float to the surface because the salt has made the water denser than the egg. Better still, you can suspend the egg half-way up the jug. Remove the egg from the jug and pour away the brine until the jug is only half full, then fill it to the top with cold water. Lower the egg into the jug once more and it should sink through the water and float on the brine in the bottom half.

The Dating Game

 **Skill Level:** ❸

YOU WILL NEED:
A CALENDAR, PENCIL AND PAPER

There are people who seem to go through their whole lives not knowing what day it is. They forget birthdays and anniversaries with monotonous regularity and even have to mark Christmas in their diary – that's if they can find their diary. If you have a box calendar (one in which each week of the month starts on a fresh line), there is a simple solution. Ask your forgetful friend to pick any month on the calendar and to draw a square around any four dates – two from one week and two from the next – without showing you. For, thanks to a cunning mathematical calculation, you are going to reveal precisely which four dates he has selected.

First tell him to add up the four numbers and to tell you the result. Let us assume that he has chosen the 8th, 9th, 15th and 16th. Therefore his total will be 48. Now you divide by 4 (to leave 12) and then subtract 4 (to make 8). This will always be the lowest of the four chosen numbers. All you have to do now is add 1 for the next date (9) and add 7 to each of these first two dates (in this case 15 and 16). Unlike your friend's memory, it never fails.

The Unstoppable Egg

 **Skill Level:** ❸

YOU WILL NEED:
A RAW EGG, A PLATE

Here's another egg trick. Spin a raw egg on a plate and gently touch it with your finger to stop it. When the egg has stopped, remove your finger and, without any assistance from you, the egg will start spinning all over again. This is because when you put your finger on the egg, you stop the shell, but inertia keeps the white and the yolk spinning. So when you let go, the moving white and yolk make the egg start to spin again. This trick won't work with a hard-boiled egg because the contents are solid. It's none too effective with scrambled egg either…

The Trick Envelope

Skill Level: ❹

YOU WILL NEED:
FIVE ENVELOPES, FIVE BUTTONS, GLUE, A BLINDFOLD

From a set of five identical envelopes, take one and glue the inside of one corner. Then sort out five buttons, all the same size, but one a different colour from the other four. After leaving the glue to set, you can start the trick. Put the envelopes in a pile with the sticky one at the bottom. Hand the top four envelopes and the four identical buttons to four friends and ask each to drop a button in their envelope and to seal it. Allow them to examine the different button, assuring them that it is the same weight, shape and size as the others, and drop it into the trick envelope, sealing it. Shuffle the envelopes, keeping all the top edges together, and ask someone to blindfold you. To your stooges, it seems impossible to detect which contains the odd button, but all you have to do is hold each envelope in turn by the top edge and shake it from side to side. In four cases, movement will be unimpaired, but in the fifth the button will be unable to roll into the glued corner. This is the envelope containing the odd button. When you have found the trick envelope, declare that this is the one holding the different-coloured button, rip off your blindfold, tear open the envelope and parade the button in front of your fawning audience.

Well, Well

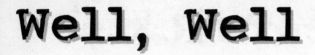 **Skill Level:** ❹

YOU WILL NEED:
A HANDKERCHIEF, A PEN

Form a circle with the thumb and forefinger of your left hand and drape a handkerchief over the top. Push a pen down into the circle to form a well in the handkerchief. Craftily open your thumb and forefinger slightly and this time push the pen down into the gap created at the side of the handkerchief next to the well. From your audience's viewpoint, it will look as if the pen is going into the well again. Pull the pen through from underneath and it will seem that the pen has gone right through the handkerchief. Then parade the intact handkerchief. It won't take everyone long to work out what you did, but you'll have enjoyed your moment of glory.

Magic Glass

🦉 **Skill Level:** ❹

YOU WILL NEED:
A GLASS OR SEE-THROUGH PLASTIC CUP, A
HANDKERCHIEF, A COIN, TWO SHEETS OF WHITE PAPER,
PENCIL, SCISSORS, GLUE

Since this trick involves putting glue round the rim of a glass, you should avoid using the finest crystal and settle instead for a glass which came as a free gift from your local garage and which has been gathering dust in the loft along with promotional ashtrays, key-rings and pens that don't work. Alternatively, you could use a plastic cup provided it's transparent. Before meeting your public, you should place your glass upside down on a piece of white paper and draw a circle around the circumference of the glass. Cut out the circle and glue it to the mouth of the glass. It should fit precisely around the rim of the glass so, if there is any excess paper, you need to trim it off. Lay out another sheet of plain white paper on a table and place the glass on the paper. If your cutting has been up to scratch, the glass's paper lid will be undetectable. Now for the trick. Ask a friend to loan you a coin and boast that you have the ability to make it disappear and reappear at will, simply by using a magic glass. Put the coin on the sheet of white paper next to the glass. Produce a handkerchief, drape it over the glass and then lift the glass with the handkerchief and place it over the coin. Mutter a magic spell – like "Liz Hurley's stripping off on the telly" (sounds magic to me) – and then remove the handkerchief. The coin seems to have disappeared although you know that it is lurking under the paper lid of the glass. If your friend looks crestfallen at having just lost 10p, assure him that there's no cause for alarm – you can magic it back just as easily. Drape the handkerchief over the glass again, say the magic words, lift the handkerchief and glass and, right on cue, the coin reappears. Your friend has kept his coin and you've kept a friend.

The Mystery Mathematician

 **Skill Level: ❹**

YOU WILL NEED:
A SMALL NOTE PAD WITH IDENTICAL FRONT AND BACK COVERS, A PENCIL, A PIECE OF PAPER

Take a small note pad, which has identical front and back covers, and on the back page write three three-digit numbers, such as 246, 759 and 333. Try to make the handwriting for each set of figures look different, suggesting that they were not written by the same person. Add the figures together (in this case 1338), write the answer on a piece of paper, seal it in an envelope and hand the envelope to someone for safe keeping. Then open the pad at the front page and ask three people each to write a three-digit number with the same pen you used. So far, so honest. Now comes the devious bit. Open the pad at the back page (where your numbers are), give it to someone completely different and ask him or her to add those numbers together. Finally ask the person with the envelope to open it and read out the number contained within. And, hey presto, they're exactly the same... because the numbers added up were the three that you wrote down originally.

The Magic Thimble

Skill Level: ④

YOU WILL NEED:
A THIMBLE, A HANDKERCHIEF

Put a thimble on the forefinger of your right hand and hold it up for all to see. Show everyone that your hand is otherwise empty. Keep your forefinger raised, but lower your remaining fingers. With your left hand, drape a handkerchief over your right, at the same time lowering your forefinger quickly and replacing it with your middle finger. Positioning your open left hand as a screen from the audience, poke your right forefinger under the edge of the handkerchief and, lowering your left palm slightly, grip the thimble in your palm and transfer it to the covered middle finger alongside. Swiftly bend the now thimble-free forefinger and sneak it back under the handkerchief. Move your left hand away and the audience will see one upright digit (your middle finger although they will still think it's your forefinger) covered by a handkerchief topped by a thimble. Unless they can find a more rational explanation, the thimble has penetrated the handkerchief. Let them examine handkerchief and thimble, both of which bear no indication of tampering. Reluctantly, they will have to conclude that you are a genius.

Egg and Bottle

Skill Level: ❹

YOU WILL NEED:
AN EGG, A BOTTLE, A PIECE OF PAPER, A MATCH OR TAPER

First you need to find a bottle with a neck marginally narrower than a cooked egg from which the shell has been removed. An empty carafe is usually about right. Now you drop a crumpled up piece of paper into the bottom of the bottle and light it, either by dropping in a burning match or by using a taper. (It is important that you follow these instructions carefully and use a taper not a tapir, since trying to light a scrap of paper with a South American hoofed mammal only creates unnecessary difficulties). Quickly, before the fire burns itself out, insert the shelled egg in an upright position so that it is wedged in the neck of the bottle. As the paper continues to burn, the egg should be sucked through the neck and into the bottle. It's all to do with the burning paper using up all the oxygen. With the egg acting as a sealant, the air pressure inside the jar is reduced and the egg sucked in. Whatever the reasons, it's a good stunt.

Step Into Christmas

Skill Level: ❹

YOU WILL NEED:
A CHRISTMAS OR BIRTHDAY CARD, A PENCIL, SCISSORS

Of all the challenges likely to be thrown at you in life, stepping through a Christmas card isn't one of them. But it's always best to be prepared and so, mindful of that, here is how you can achieve the seemingly impossible. Take an ordinary greetings card (it doesn't have to be Christmas) and, keeping it closed, draw a dozen or so straight lines back and forth across the card. Line 1 should touch side A, but not side B; line 2 should touch side B, but not side A; line 3 should touch side A, but not side B; and so on with only alternate lines reaching the same edge of the card. Then carefully cut along the lines and open out the card. Now cut along the fold down the centre of the shredded card, taking care not to cut the strips of card at either end. Finally open the whole thing out and you should have created a circle of joined card large enough for you to step through.

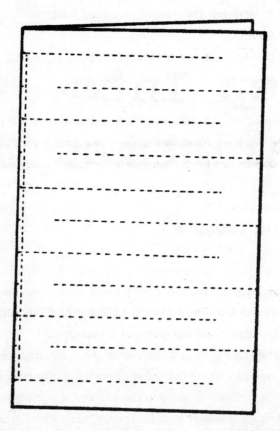

The Floating Needle

Skill Level: ❹

YOU WILL NEED:
A BOWL OF WATER, A SEWING NEEDLE, A TABLE FORK

This may not be the grandest magic feat ever witnessed – it is doubtful whether Houdini made his name with it – but a bit of dry ice and a roll of drums can do wonders for the most ordinary trick. Anyway making metal float on water is quite impressive in its own way. Take a small bowl and fill it with clean water. Then rest a sewing needle across the prongs of a table fork and very gently lower the fork onto the water, barely breaking the surface. As you take the fork slowly away, the needle should float. If you really want to know why, it's because, although the fork breaks the "skin" on the water's surface, the skin quickly forms again under the needle to prevent it from sinking. The art of this trick is to be gentle with the fork. Any heavy-handedness will assuredly end in heartbreak.

The Magic Book

 **Skill Level:** ❹

YOU WILL NEED:
A HARD-BACK BOOK, EIGHT 5P COINS

For this trick, you need a hard-back book that has a little tunnel in the spine when you open it out flat. The tunnel must be wide enough to allow a 5p coin to slide in and out. When nobody is looking, slip a 5p coin into the tunnel. Place the book on a flat surface so that the coin doesn't fall out and count out another seven 5p coins to your audience. Make sure they can see that you have no other coins secreted about your person – under a thumb, up a sleeve, between fillings. Opening the book somewhere near the centre, ask your chosen stooge to place the seven coins in a row down the middle of the book. Close the book carefully, keeping it horizontal, and ask the stooge to hold his or her hands out. Then tip the coins into their waiting hands and watch for the look of amazement as the seven coins have turned into eight. Amid the avalanche of coins (rather like winning on a slot machine), nobody will notice that the extra coin has come from the spine of the book.

The Double Balloon

Skill Level: ⑤

YOU WILL NEED:
TWO DIFFERENT-COLOURED BALLOONS, A PIN

Stun your friends by changing the colour of a balloon before their very eyes. To carry off this amazing feat, you need to blow up two different-coloured balloons, one inside the other. Since you don't want anyone to know there is a second balloon, it makes sense to have a darker colour on the outside (red) with a paler colour (yellow) inside. Now announce that you are going to burst the balloon and make it change colour. Stick a pin in the outer red balloon, snatch the wizened remains, hide them in your hand and you are left with the still-inflated inner yellow balloon. The speed of the operation should be such that nobody spots the skin of the red balloon disappearing into your hand.

Raise the Bottle

 **Skill Level:** ❺

YOU WILL NEED:
A DRINKING STRAW, A BOTTLE

The challenge here is to pick up an empty bottle without touching it, using nothing more than an ordinary drinking straw. The trick is to bend the straw back on itself at a point just over half the way up. Push the bent bit into the bottle and, with any luck, it will wedge itself against the side of the bottle, enabling you to lift it up gently. Position a couple of slip fielders, though, just in case it doesn't work.

Evaporated
Milk

Skill Level: ⑤

YOU WILL NEED:
A GLASS, WHITE PAPER, CARDBOARD, GLUE

The vanishing glass of milk always looks good on stage or on TV and therein lies its secret. For this is a trick which should not be attempted close-up, unless your audience are direct descendants of Mr Magoo. So position the table several feet away from the spectators and cover it with a tablecloth large enough to reach down to the floor at the back of the table, thus providing a screen. There are other things you need to do beforehand. First you must find an ordinary glass tumbler or indeed a plastic one, as long as it is transparent. Take a rectangular piece of cardboard and roll it into a tube so that it not only fits neatly over the glass, but is also slightly taller than it. Glue the edges of the tube together for that professional look. Next find a sheet of white paper and roll this into a tube which fits perfectly inside the glass. It should be an inch or two shorter than the glass and must reach right down to the bottom. Since this white paper is going to play the part of the non-existent milk, make sure you keep the join away from the audience's view. When you have completed your preparations, it's showtime. Stand the glass with the white paper inside it on the table. Don't move the glass around or some bright spark will cotton on to the fact that the milk is solidified. Show the cardboard tube to everyone so that they can see there's nothing hidden inside and place it over the glass of "milk". Now announce that you are going to make the milk disappear. Utter a few magic words and lift the cardboard tube up from the glass, at the same time using your fingers to pull the white paper clear too. As everyone reacts in astonishment, momentarily rest the cardboard tube on the back edge of the table, allowing the paper to fall to the floor (its descent hidden from the audience by the tablecloth). Keeping hold of the cardboard tube, pull it towards you and pass it and the glass around so that everyone can check that there is nothing untoward about either item. If only they knew...

The Swinging Vase

Skill Level: 5

YOU WILL NEED:

A SMALL, NARROW-NECKED VASE, A LENGTH OF ROPE, A SMALL RUBBER BALL OR RUBBER ERASER

Warning: This trick could be dangerous. Take care!

No matter how enthusiastic you are about certain tricks, it is hardly worth destroying family heirlooms to perform them. Just as you wouldn't play noughts and crosses on a Rembrandt or make a doorstop out of a Chippendale, so you shouldn't use a half-decent vase for this trick. So put the Ming away and opt instead for some ghastly ornament which is destined for the next car boot sale. You also need a small rubber ball or a rubber eraser, the size of which is solely dependent on that of the neck of the vase. For the ball or eraser must be large enough to wedge itself in the neck of the vase, but small enough to pass through the neck with a gentle shove. In general terms, the smaller the vase the better. To prepare for the trick, push the ball or eraser through the neck into the bottom of the vase. Since the rubber item must not be seen by the audience, don't choose a cut glass vase. Explain that you are going to perform the amazing Swinging Vase trick whereby an ordinary vase will be suspended in mid-air by an ordinary length of rope. Show everyone the piece of rope, which should be about 1ft long, so that they can see that there's no Blu-tack or chewing gum stuck to the end and then lower part of the rope into the vase. Next turn the vase upside down. Do this quickly so that nobody can hear the ball or eraser rattling around inside. If all goes well, the hidden ball should roll into the neck and wedge the rope firmly in place so that when you let go of the rope, it will hang from the neck of the vase. Just to make sure, tug the rope towards you a little. This should pull the ball further into the neck. Now for the moment of truth. Turn the vase the right way up again, let go of the vase entirely and only hold on to the end of the rope. You should now be able to use the rope to swing the vase back and forth. Everyone will be mightily impressed, but you still need to conclude matters without giving the game away. So as you pull the rope out, cup your hand over the mouth of the vase and allow the ball to drop into your palm. Keep the rubber ball hidden in your fist and then slip it into your pocket while allowing your fans to inspect the vase and rope.

Balloon Switch

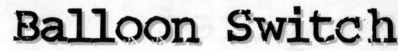 **Skill Level: 5**

YOU WILL NEED:
FOUR BALLOONS (TWO OF EACH COLOUR), TWO PAPER
BAGS, A PENCIL

Here is another balloon baffler. Prepare for it by acquiring four balloons, two of each colour (say purple and green) and, using something like the blunt end of a pencil, push one purple balloon inside one of the green balloons and vice-versa. Don't inflate the balloons and make sure that in both cases you leave the tip of the inner balloon protruding. Now take two ordinary brown paper bags and on the outside of one bag write "purple" and on the other write "green". Hold the balloons by the neck so that the protruding tips of the inner balloons are concealed from the audience. All they can see is one deflated purple balloon and one deflated green balloon. Allow everyone to inspect the bags for booby traps and then, still keeping the necks hidden, drop the purple balloon into the bag marked "purple" and the green balloon into the bag marked "green". To gasps of disbelief, declare that you are about to make the purple balloon jump into the green bag and the green balloon perform similar somersaults into the purple bag. Blow on the purple bag and, gripping it by the sides so that you have a firm hold on the balloon, pull out the inner green balloon by its neck. Wave it aloft to the audience, quickly crumpling the bag and the purple balloon contained within. Repeat the procedure with the green bag, pulling out the purple balloon to prove that the two balloons have swapped bags just as you promised.

Recycled Paper

 **Skill Level: 5**

YOU WILL NEED:
TWO PAPER TISSUES, A BOX OF MATCHES, AN ASHTRAY

In these days of conservation and green issues, recycling is an important issue. And nothing makes you think "green" more than a paper tissue, particularly if it's been used a lot. With this trick, you achieve every Amazon Rain Forest PR man's dream by appearing to make a burnt-out tissue rise from the ashes and become new again. If only it were that simple. For sad to say there is no simple solution – the trick relies upon the use of a second hidden tissue masquerading as the original. The audience see you hold up a perfectly ordinary tissue. On the table are an ashtray and a half-open matchbox, containing, not unreasonably, a few matches. But only you know that the box is half open for a very good reason because secreted in the sleeve of the box behind the tray is the second paper tissue. Next you crumple the first tissue and put it in the ashtray. Placing the palm of your right hand at the rear of the matchbox, you pluck out a match with your left hand and strike it against the side of the box. Everybody's eyes will be on the lit match which means that they probably won't pay much attention to you shutting the box, a movement which pushes the second tissue into your right hand. As soon as this happens, you clench your right fist and then set fire to the first tissue in the ashtray. After that tissue has been reduced to a cinder, you reach your right hand into the charred remains, rummage around and open your hand to reveal a perfectly recycled tissue.

The Knotted Handkerchief

 **Skill Level:** ⑤

**YOU WILL NEED:
A HANDKERCHIEF**

When worn on the head, the knotted handkerchief is one of the great fashion accessories of the British seaside holidaymaker. You can see them every heatwave on promenades from Blackpool to Bognor, as much a part of the scenery as donkey rides, kiss-me-quick hats and dodgy hamburgers. The knotted handkerchief is also the end product of this trick as you challenge all-comers that they won't be able to tie a knot in an ordinary handkerchief without letting go of the ends. The theory is straightforward enough. You fold one corner of the handkerchief across to the opposite corner and then fold your arms in front of you. Keep your hands in this position and pick up the ends of the handkerchief. Maintaining your grip on the ends of the handkerchief, unfold your arms and you should finish up with a knot in the middle of the handkerchief. But don't bet your mortgage on it until you've practised it a few times.

Rolling Pin

 **Skill Level:** ⑤

YOU WILL NEED:
A SAFETY PIN, A HANDKERCHIEF,

Spread a handkerchief out on a table and fasten a safety pin near the edge of the handkerchief which is closest to you. Roll the safety pin over to the left three times, the result being that the handkerchief also rolls over. Press your left hand firmly on the handkerchief to keep it in place and hold the protruding end of the pin between the thumb and forefinger of your right hand. Now pull down sharply and the pin comes away without tearing the handkerchief even though it is still closed. You may need to practice this, though.

The Sliding Pencil

 **Skill Level: ❺**

YOU WILL NEED:
A PENCIL, A SCARF, A JACKET

You need to wrap up for this game, not only because there'll be a chill in the air if you get it wrong, but because a jacket is a definite requirement. Hold a pencil up and allow everyone to inspect it for authenticity. Once they are satisfied that it is definitely an ordinary pencil and not some cunning disguise like an HB stick insect, hold the pencil in your right hand and cover it with a scarf. Magicians usually favour brightly coloured silk scarves, but if all you can lay your hands on is a Mansfield Town scarf or the Rupert Bear one that Granny Vera knitted you last Christmas, that will have to do. With the scarf draped over pencil and hand, thrust your forefinger stiffly skywards so that the audience will assume that it is the pencil poking into the material. At the same time, allow the pencil to slide into the sleeve of your jacket. Remove the scarf and, would you believe it, the pencil has vanished.

Changing the Cutlery

Skill Level: 8

YOU WILL NEED:
A SPOON, A FORK, A TABLE NAPKIN, A TABLECLOTH

Cover the table with a cloth and place a spoon on the cloth. Lay out a table napkin in a diamond shape so that the centre of the napkin covers the spoon. On top of the napkin and directly above the spoon, put a fork. Fold the corner nearest you (corner A) over to the opposite corner (corner B), leaving it an inch or so short. Attribute this to carelessness rather any pre-conceived plan, but the shortfall ensures that the spoon remains hidden beneath the napkin. Hold the two concealed items of cutlery through the napkin with both hands and roll the napkin back towards you (the tablecloth will muffle the sound of the spoon) until corner A has made one complete rotation of the tightened roll. Both corners will now protrude from the roll. Placing one finger firmly on corner A, pull corner B sharply towards you and, by magic, the fork has changed into a spoon. Gather up the evidence before anyone realizes that the fork is now beneath the rolled-up napkin.

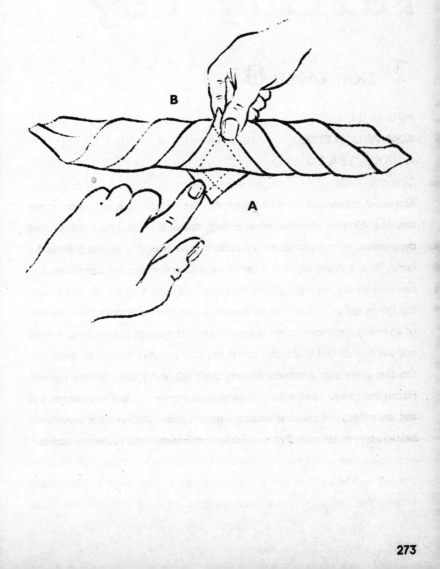

Catch a Falling Key

 **Skill Level: ⑤**

YOU WILL NEED:
A KEY, A TEA TOWEL

The most important item of equipment for this trick is not listed above because it's the services of a willing assistant who has been primed beforehand as to what to do. Make sure your friends are sitting around a table. Take a single key and a tea towel and drape the tea towel over the key. Pick up the key through the tea towel and hold it up for all to see. Grip the key at either end so that its presence is clearly reflected in the position of your fingers. Now lower the towel over the lap of one of your friends and ask her to feel under the towel and confirm that the key is still there. Do the same with a second person. Both will verify that the key remains under the towel. Then select, apparently at random, a third volunteer, but this time it is your clandestine accomplice. Once again hold the towel over her lap, but make sure that the sides of the towel reach down to her legs so that a screen is formed. As she reaches underneath, she gently removes the key and hides it in her lap. For their part, your fingers, which were holding the key, stay in the same position, implying that the key is still beneath the towel. After your accomplice has confirmed that the key is still there, you suddenly whip the towel into the air and reveal that the key has vanished. But that's only part of the trick. For now you promise to make the key return. Position your fingers as before over the towel as if the key is underneath and return to your assistant. Once again hold the towel over her lap so that the sides act as a screen and ask her to feel whether the key has reappeared. As she reaches under the towel, she simply replaces the key and exclaims her astonishment. You then pull away the tea towel to show that the key has materialized again, just as you promised it would.

Penetration

 **Skill Level: ⑥**

YOU WILL NEED:
THREE POLYSTYRENE CUPS, TWO PAPER PELLETS

By the simple act of tapping your finger, you will appear to make a small paper pellet pass through an ordinary polystyrene cup to the table below. The catch is that one of the cups already contains a hidden paper pellet. Begin by finding a colourful page in a magazine and tear off sufficient to make two paper pellets. These should be of the same size and colour. Take three polystyrene cups and put one of the paper pellets inside one of the cups. Stack the three cups on the table, mouth side up, ensuring that the one with the hidden pellet is in the middle. So to the performance. After explaining your intentions, show the audience the base of each cup so that they can see there are no holes. Then invert each of the cups in turn and line them up on the table. This should be done smoothly and swiftly so that nobody is able to see the hidden pellet. The cup containing the pellet should be in the middle of the row of three. As a result of the inversion, the pellet is now, of course, underneath the cup. Pick up the other paper pellet and put it on top of that centre cup before stacking the remaining two cups on top. So you now have a stack of three polystyrene cups and all the audience know is that there is a paper pellet on top of the bottom one. Tap your finger on the top cup and announce that you will make that pellet force its way through to the table. Lift off all three cups and there indeed is the pellet on the table beneath the bottom cup.

Magazine
Magic

Skill Level: ❻

YOU WILL NEED:
NINE MAGAZINES, PENCIL AND PAPER

This is one of the more expensive tricks in this book because you need nine magazines. You might be able to borrow three from the doctor's waiting room (if you don't mind a pre-decimalization issue of *Woman's Realm* extolling the virtues of Oxydol and Tide), but the remaining six must be three pairs of duplicates so you will probably need to buy those. If possible, the six different magazines should each have highly distinctive covers so that they are easily recognizable. To prepare for this mind-reading extravaganza, you need to remove the covers from the three duplicate magazines and replace them with the covers from three of the different ones so that you are left with six magazines, all with different covers, but the copy inside three of them is identical with that of the other three! Make a mental note of which pairs of covers contain the same material. Now that your preparation is complete, you can display your mind-reading prowess. Hold up the six magazines and point out that they are all different which, of course, the audience can see for themselves by the covers. But don't let them inspect the magazines or they might become a shade suspicious to find that a cover of Philately Monthly contains a copy of Loaded! Even an explanation that it is a special edition of Philately Monthly in which stamp collectors nominated their favourite sexual fantasies is unlikely to convince. Ask one of your friends to pick any of the magazines and to think of a two-digit number, and tell it to you. This, you explain, will denote the page number, line and word. So if he chooses 26, this will be the sixth word on the second line of page 26. To underline this, casually pick up the magazine which you know to be identical to the one which your friend has selected. As you explain how it works, you turn to page 26 of this duplicate magazine and silently remember the sixth word on the second line, emphasizing that this demonstration is merely to reiterate the rules of engagement. When you have done that, put down the magazine and ask your friend to concentrate hard on the word. Say that when your friend's thoughts are transferred in your direction, you will write down the word. Duly write down the word you remembered from the duplicate and fold the slip of paper. Then ask him to name the word, at which you open out the paper and reveal the very same word. Uncanny.

Upright Corks

 **Skill Level:** ❻

YOU WILL NEED:
SIX CORKS, A BOWL OF WATER

When dropped in water, corks naturally tend to float on their side so the trick here is to get six corks to float upright. The secret is to hold all six corks together in an upright cluster. Dip them in the bowl of water and hold them submerged for two minutes so that they are thoroughly soaked. If you then raise them gently to the surface, they should stay upright.

Polo

Skill Level: 6

YOU WILL NEED:
TWO POLO MINTS, A PIECE OF STRING, A PENCIL, A
HANDKERCHIEF

With a Polo mint hidden in your right hand, give one of your friends another Polo mint and a length of string and ask him to pass the string through the mint and then to hold the two ends of the string. Now that the Polo is perched astride the string, challenge anyone to remove the mint from the string without cutting the string or letting go of the ends. Of course, nobody will be able to manage it, but you insist that the solution rests with a handkerchief and a pencil. Let the spectators see that both items are perfectly ordinary and then drape the handkerchief over the mint on the string. Slide both hands under the handkerchief and place the second mint (the one hidden in your right hand) on the string and insert the pencil between it and the string. The presence of the pencil causes the mint to be held in place even though it is not attached to the string. Then put one hand over the first mint, drag it along to the end of the string and take both ends from the volunteer. As you do so, conceal the mint in your hand. Holding both ends of the string, you claim that if your volunteer were now to remove the handkerchief and the pencil, the mint would be released from the string... and that is precisely what happens. Everyone looks puzzled and you eat the evidence.

The Word

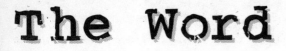 **Skill Level: ❻**

YOU WILL NEED:
A THICK PAPERBACK BOOK, A BUSINESS CARD

This is another impressive exhibition of mind-reading, performed with a thick paperback book and a business card. Show the book to one of your friends and ask him to flick through it to verify that it is the genuine article and has not been tampered with in any way. Underline the fact that there are a couple of hundred pages and a few hundred words on each page. This will make your eventual revelation seem all the more incredible. Ask your volunteer to scan the book, to choose any page and to insert a business card at that page. Before he hands the book back to you, tell him to remember the page number and also the last word on that page. By sheer concentration, you will name both the chosen page number and the last word on it. Holding the book in your hand, flick through the pages as if you are innocently emphasizing just how many pages and words there are. The presence of the business card will cause your thumb to jump at that page, allowing you a split second to make a mental note of the page number and the last word before you continue apace through the rest of the book. Obviously you need to practise this action so that it looks smooth and undetectable. If you pause for an eternity at the chosen page or have to put glasses on, it rather detracts from the element of surprise. When you have finished leafing through the pages, ask your volunteer to concentrate hard on the page number and final word. After appearing to struggle for a few moments (a hint of fallibility always makes the performance seem more genuine), rejoice in the news that your volunteer's thoughts have been successfully transferred to you and reveal the answers. While you're at it, you could mention that you've picked up on another of his thoughts. Does his girlfriend know that he fancies the barmaid at the Nag's Head?

The Torn
Tissue

Skill Level: ❻

YOU WILL NEED:
TWO PAPER TISSUES

Prepare for this trick by folding a paper tissue six times until you are left with just one-64th of the original surface area. Press the squashed tissue against one corner of another ordinary tissue and grip it firmly in place between the thumb and forefinger of your left hand. Hold the unfolded tissue aloft, keeping the folded one hidden at the back, and announce that you are going to rip the paper tissue into strips and then magically restore it. Keeping the folded tissue in place with your left hand, start tearing the other tissue into strips with your right hand. When you have torn everything except the corner where the folded tissue is hidden, gather all the pieces in your left hand and blow on it as magicians are wont to do. Then with your right hand, reach into the torn pieces and pull out the folded tissue, allowing it to open up in your hand. At the same time keep the torn strips hidden in your left hand. To those who are easily pleased, it will look as if you have restored the torn tissue.

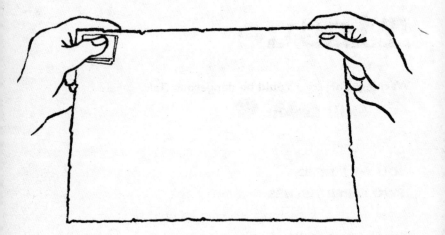

Swing the Bucket

 **Skill Level: ❻**

YOU WILL NEED:
A BUCKET OF WATER

Warning: This trick could be dangerous. Take care!

Half fill a bucket with water and swing it in a full circle. If you make the bucket swing fast enough, none of the water will spill out. The reason is suitably scientific. As the bucket is swung around, it is constantly forced to change direction, but the water inside still attempts to travel in straight lines. As a result, the water is pressed against the interior of the bucket and can't escape. For obvious reasons, it is best to demonstrate this trick in the garden.

The Vanishing Coin

Skill Level: ❻

YOU WILL NEED:
A HANDKERCHIEF, A SMALL PIECE OF DOUBLE-SIDED STICKY TAPE, A 10P PIECE

That staple of magic tricks, the handkerchief, is required again as you demonstrate the art of making money disappear quicker than a vengeful wife with a cheating husband's credit card. To prepare for this trick, you need to stick a small piece of double-sided sticky tape across one corner of a handkerchief. Then show a 10p coin and the handkerchief to your audience, holding the handkerchief in such a way that the sticky tape is concealed by your hand. Lay the handkerchief on a flat surface with the taped corner nearest to you and place the coin in the centre of the handkerchief. Fold over the taped corner to the centre and press it firmly on to the coin, repeating the process with the other three corners. Utter some form of magic spell ("Hocus Pocus", "Abracadabra", "Una Paloma Blanca" or whatever) and lift up the last corner to unfold the handkerchief, ensuring that the side with the coin is facing away from the audience. Finally pick up the handkerchief by two corners, including the one with the coin now stuck there, to reveal that the coin has vanished completely... because your finger and thumb are covering the coin.

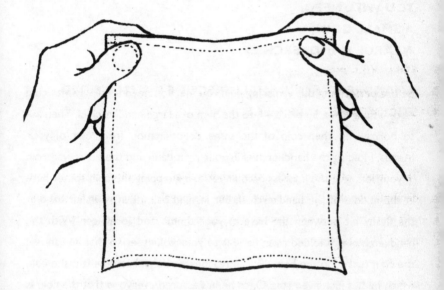

Hemmed In

Skill Level: ⑥

YOU WILL NEED:
A SMALL COIN,
A LARGE HANDKERCHIEF

Before performing this vanishing coin routine, you need to slip a small coin
– something like a 5p piece – into the hem of a large handkerchief. Then ask
to borrow another coin of the same denomination from one of your
friends. Holding the handkerchief in your right hand and the borrowed coin
in your left, give the impression that you are wrapping the coin somewhere
in the middle of the handkerchief, but instead palm it in your left hand at
the fleshy bit between the base of your thumb and forefinger. With the
handkerchief still folded over, hand it to your volunteer so that he can feel
the coin tucked in the hem. Not unreasonably, he will assume it is the coin
which he has just given you. Once he has assured everyone that the coin is
still wrapped in the handkerchief, you announce that you will make the 5p
disappear. Whip one corner of the handkerchief through the air in your
most theatrical manner and hold up both sides for all to see. It will seem
that the coin has vanished although, unless your handkerchief has got loose
stitching, it will still be tucked safely in the hem.

The Unbroken Match

 **Skill Level: ⑥**

YOU WILL NEED:
A LARGE HANDKERCHIEF OR TABLE NAPKIN WITH A HEM, A BOX OF MATCHES, A PEN

To set up this trick, you need to slip a match unseen into the hem of a napkin (or large handkerchief) and make sure that it stays in place. And don't forget in which part of the napkin the match is hidden. You then produce a box of matches and ask someone to pick a match and to mark it with a pen so that it is clearly identifiable. Open out the napkin so that everybody can see that it is empty and fold it over the selected match. Now you need to bring the first hidden match into play, casually manoeuvring the napkin so that the match in the hem is roughly in the middle of the folded napkin. When it is in position, ask your volunteer to feel the match through the napkin and to break it in half. You then shake the napkin in the air, open it out and the unbroken match falls to the floor. The person checks the match for her pen mark and is stunned to find that it is indeed the match she chose earlier.

With This Ring

Skill Level: 7

YOU WILL NEED:
A SMALL RING, A PIECE OF STRING, A LARGE
HANDKERCHIEF

Take a piece of string, about a metre and a half (5ft) long, and show it to the assembled throng. Then produce a wedding ring or, if you don't want to risk losing the ring, a metal washer – unless of course you bought the ring from a market stall, in which case the washer is probably more valuable. Fold the string in half and push the loop through the ring. Push the two ends of the string through the loop and pull them tight. Holding the ring in one hand, ask a volunteer to clasp the two ends of the string. Pick up a handkerchief and drop it over the hand holding the ring. Put your free hand under the handkerchief, in such a way that the ring remains hidden from view, loosen the string a little and slide the loop over the ring, thus freeing ring from string. Finally ask your volunteer to pull the string and, as he or she does so, the empty string emerges from beneath the handkerchief and you are left holding the ring.

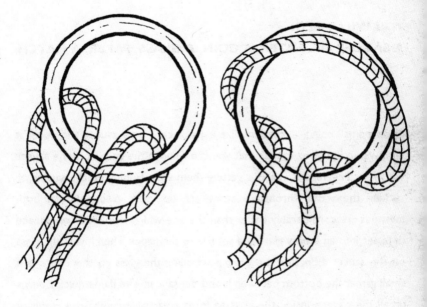

High and Dry

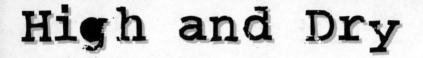 **Skill Level:** ❼

YOU WILL NEED:
A SAUCER OF WATER, A COIN, A GLASS, PAPER, A MATCH

Place a small coin – something like a 1p piece – on a saucer and cover it with water. Bet your friends that you can remove the coin from the saucer with your fingers, but without getting them wet. Tipping up the saucer or sucking the water through a straw are not permitted although both methods are considerably easier than the one which follows. Drop a piece of paper into an empty glass and set fire to the paper. Then invert the glass on the saucer alongside the coin, positioning the glass so that there is a small gap at the bottom between it and the saucer. The flame quickly burns up all the oxygen inside the glass to form a partial vacuum, as a result of which the water is sucked into the glass, leaving the coin high and dry on the saucer. Simply pick up the coin to win the bet.

Money to Burn

Skill Level: ⑦

YOU WILL NEED:
AN ENVELOPE, A BANKNOTE, A BOX OF MATCHES,
AN ASHTRAY, A PEN

If you are blessed with a sadistic streak, you'll love this trick where you watch an innocent volunteer squirm with discomfort at the thought that you have destroyed his hard-earned cash. Maybe in the hands of Paul Daniels or Wayne Dobson, he would be confident that the note would somehow reappear intact, but with a novice like you he's not so sure. His fears may not be groundless, so practise this a few times with a slip of paper instead of a banknote until you get the hang of it. To prepare for the trick, you need to make a small slit, about an inch and a half long, in the address side of an ordinary white envelope. Place the envelope flap side up on the table so that the slit is hidden from view. Arrange an ashtray adjacent to the envelope. Also put a box of matches in your left trouser pocket. Start proceedings by borrowing a banknote (the higher the denomination the better) from a reluctant volunteer and ask him to sign it clearly with a pen for future identification. Show the note to the audience so that everyone can see the telltale mark. Fold the note in half three times so that you end up with a small packet. Pick up the envelope with your left hand in such a way that your fingers cover the slit and with your right hand, pull back the flap and push in the banknote so that part of it passes through the slit to the outside of the envelope. Making sure that the protruding note and the slit are still concealed by your fingers, seal the envelope. Next transfer the envelope from your left hand to your right, using the fingers of your left hand to drag the protruding note into the palm of your hand where it must remain hidden. With your right hand, place the envelope flap side up on the table once again. Meanwhile reach your left hand into your trouser pocket, deposit the banknote there and pull out the box of matches. Hold the envelope over the ashtray, showing the flap side to the audience, and set fire to it with a match. When the envelope has been reduced to a pile of cinders, rummage through the debris with a horrified look which strongly implies that the banknote has not survived its ordeal. Offer profuse apologies, promising to get it right next time, and ask your volunteer whether there is anything he would like by way of recompense – maybe the signed photo of Anne Robinson from your collection of celebrity winkers. Now that he is almost certainly incandescent with rage, agree that you'll have to reimburse him financially. Retrieve the banknote from your pocket, open it out and hand it to him. As he takes it, point out the signature. While he stands mouth ajar at the realization that it is his note, hold it up so that everyone else can see what a clever boy you are.

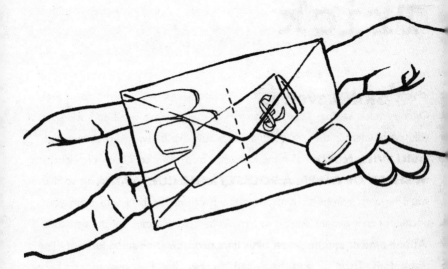

The Tablecloth Trick

 **Skill Level:** ❼

YOU WILL NEED:
A SHEET OF PAPER, A POLYSTYRENE CUP, WATER

At one time or another, most of us have probably tried some form of "The Tablecloth Trick"… and have had to pay for the broken crockery afterwards. It all looks so easy on TV. The table is laden with glasses, plates, cups, saucers and bottles and the magician saunters up, gives the tablecloth one sharp tug and it comes away in his hand, leaving all of the glassware and china standing in place. Not a crack or a chip in sight. The trick works thanks to our old friend inertia, but is still notoriously difficult for an amateur to get right. So rather than risk a future of having to eat off newspaper and drink out of the dog's bowl, practise first on a scaled-down version involving a sheet of paper and a polystyrene cup half-filled with water. Put the sheet of paper on the table so that the very end overlaps the edge of the table and place the cup on top of the paper, making sure that the paper is completely dry. If any of the water spills from the cup on to the paper, the trick won't work. Now for the tug. It must be swift and sharp – any hesitation will prove fatal. At the moment you pull, the paper must also be kept flat and not raised, which is why it is a good idea to position it so that it overlaps the table. If you manage to perfect it, you can move on to more ambitious projects, but resist the temptation to try "The Tablecloth Trick" in a posh restaurant. Successful or not, the waiter is unlikely to see the funny side.

 Loop the Loop

 **Skill Level: ❼**

YOU WILL NEED:
TWO LENGTHS OF STRING

To make this trick work, you need to cut two pieces of string of vastly differing lengths. The short piece must be able to fit inside your mouth without you looking like "The Godfather", so around four inches should be about right for the average-sized orifice. The other piece can be three or four times longer. Before confronting your audience, you need to loop the short piece and the long piece together and cover the loop with your thumb. The first thing the audience will see is you holding in your right hand what appear to be two parallel pieces of string of the same length. What they don't know is that your thumb is concealing the loop linking the two pieces and that consequently the two top ends belong to one piece of string and the two bottom ends to the other piece. Tell the audience that you are going to make the two lengths join into one and that the only way to do that is to apply a touch of magic spit (this will have the added advantage of making some people turn away in disgust, rendering them unable to witness your sleight of mouth). Suck on the two top ends and bring your right hand up to your mouth so that it not only hides the loop, but also the fact that you are about to put the whole of the shorter piece into your mouth. With the loop broken, you pull the long piece free and, in the eyes of the audience, the two lengths have joined up. The shorter piece meanwhile remains in your mouth while you pray that nobody asks you to make a victory speech.

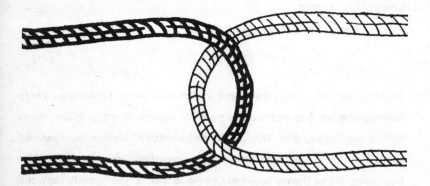

A Tale of Two Bags

 **Skill Level: 7**

YOU WILL NEED:
TWO IDENTICAL PAPER BAGS, A PAPER TISSUE,
CONFETTI, SCISSORS, GLUE

Find two paper bags of the same size and colour. Trim a strip all the way around the top of one bag and make a few holes in the bottom. Leave the second bag intact and sprinkle some confetti inside it. Put the first bag inside the second and glue the outer top edge of the first bag to the inner top edge of the second so that the two bags are stuck together. Show the audience the result of your hard work – what appears to be an ordinary paper bag. Tip it upside down so that they can see it is empty and pop in a paper tissue. Tell everyone that you are going to make the tissue undergo a remarkable transformation. Using all the strength you can muster, blow up the bag and burst it. As a result of the holes in the first bag, only the second outer bag will burst, allowing the confetti to fall to the floor. With you hiding the crumpled bags and the tissue in your hand, it will look as if the plain white tissue has turned to coloured confetti.

The Madness of King Edward

 **Skill Level: ❼**

YOU WILL NEED:
A SMALL POTATO, A COCKTAIL STICK, TWO FORKS, A
LENGTH OF STRING

Here is an unbelievable opportunity to re-enact the career of Blondin, the famous French tightrope walker, using a potato. Simply stretch a piece of string between two chair legs so that it is taut like a tightrope and instruct your potato (the smaller the better) to go out there and balance on the string. No potato in its right mind would attempt such a feat, but with the aid of two forks and a cocktail stick it can be done. And, in the immortal words of Jimmy Young, this is what you do. Press the cocktail stick into the potato and make a notch in the other end of the stick so that it can stand upright on the string. Holding it in place, stick the prongs of the forks into the potato (one on each side) with the handles hanging down and you will find that the contraption balances because its centre of gravity is below the string.

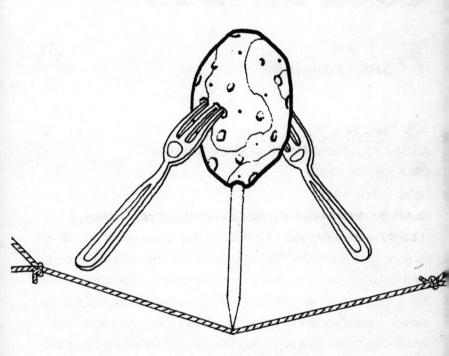

The
Secret Slit

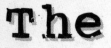 **Skill Level: 7**

YOU WILL NEED:
A STRAW, A LENGTH OF STRING, SCISSORS
OR A SHARP KNIFE

Prepare for this exhibition by making a two-inch vertical cut along one side of a drinking straw. The incision should be made approximately half-way up the straw and will be invisible to spectators. When everyone is sitting comfortably, you can begin. Thread a piece of string along the straw so that it protrudes at either end. Give it a little tug so that they can see there is just one piece of string. Put your right hand over the centre of the straw and bend it sharply in half at the slit. Make sure that the slit is on the inside of the bend. Gently pull on the lower end of the string to force it into the slit. Keep the straw tightly folded in half so that nobody can see the slit or the loose string and then cut the straw at the bend above the string. Everyone should still be able to see the string protruding from either end of the straw so they will naturally expect the string to have been cut in two. But when you straighten out the straw and blow on it magically, you are able to brandish the string intact.

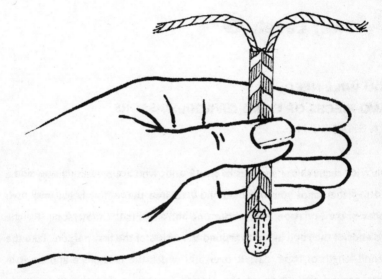

A Knotty Problem

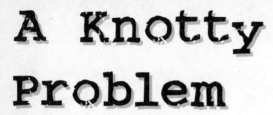 **Skill Level: ❼**

YOU WILL NEED:
TWO PIECES OF CORD OR ROPE

This trick requires the services of two friends who are perfectly happy to be tied together until you work out how to free them. You begin with two pieces of cord or rope, each about one and a half metres (5ft) long. Tie the two ends of the rope in knots around the wrists of the first person. Take the second length of rope, pass it over and under the first piece and tie it in knots around the wrists of the second person, leaving the two people suitably entwined. Tell them to try and free themselves without undoing any knots. This will prove spectacularly impossible so put them out of their misery and show them how it's done. Take the centre of the first person's rope and thread it through the noose around the wrist of the other person, the first rope passing between the knot of the second rope and the wrist. Pull the first rope to make the loop bigger and pass it over the second person's hand. Then pull the loop along and pass it through the other side of the wrist noose. Finally pull the rope right through the noose and, all being well, the two ropes should separate. And if not, there's always tomorrow…

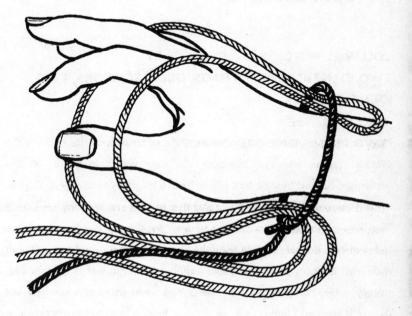

The Cut Tie

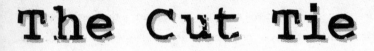 **Skill Level:** ❼

YOU WILL NEED:
TWO IDENTICAL PAPER BAGS, GLUE, SCISSORS, TWO IDENTICAL TIES

Magicians thrive on humiliation. Indeed one of their favourite tricks is the cut tie routine where a spectator can only watch in horror as the performer cuts his best tie into pieces before magically restoring it. You can try this yourself by using similar apparatus to that required for "A Tale of Two Bags". Take two identical paper bags, trim the top two inches off one and glue one side of it inside the other bag. From the outside you are left with what appears to be one paper bag, but hidden inside is another bag, giving you two compartments instead of one. The other items you need for this trick are two identical ties, one to be hidden in the bag, the other to be worn by the victim. Consequently you need to come to some arrangement with the victim beforehand, explaining what is going to happen and that he must look suitably distraught as you shred his new tie. So your starting position is one tie in the bag (under no circumstances must you allow anyone to inspect the bag), a pair of scissors in your pocket and the other tie around your friend's neck. Everyone else may be shocked to see him wearing a tie as opposed to a sweatshirt and this will give him the opportunity to lay it on thick about what a lovely tie it is, how he saw it in the shop yesterday and couldn't resist it, and that he thinks he'll wear it for ever more, even in bed. This will make its destruction all the more poignant in the eyes of the rest of your entourage. After he has waxed lyrical about his neckwear, you quietly produce the scissors from your pocket and, with an assassin-like iciness, cut his tie into pieces. Everyone, your victim included, will look aghast. What could have prompted such action? Was it because he beat you at Snakes and Ladders the other night or because he stole your last Rolo? You refuse to comment, silently placing the pieces of tie into the bag in the compartment next to the whole tie. As your friends plead with you to be reasonable about this feud, you finally relent and promise to get him a new tie. It won't take a second, you say. Close the bag, pronounce a magic spell and pull out the intact tie from its compartment, leaving the cut one inside the bag. You then hand him the restored tie against a backdrop of stunned silence.

The Invisible Tear

 **Skill Level: 8**

YOU WILL NEED:
A HANDKERCHIEF, A LARGE SAFETY PIN

It may not exactly have been your life's ambition to slide a safety pin along a handkerchief without ripping it to shreds, but it is nevertheless quite an achievement. Fold the handkerchief in half and ask someone to hold one end of the fold firmly while you grip the other. Keeping the handkerchief as taut as possible, put a safety pin (the bigger the better) through both layers just below the fold. Make sure that the non-opening bar of the safety pin is to your left. Close the pin and, with your other hand, hold the base tightly and pull the whole pin sharply down and along to the right. This has the effect of pushing the cloth up and around the point inside the cap. Slide the safety pin a little way along the handkerchief and then suddenly force the point up through the cloth again. Despite the unnerving sound of tearing, the closed safety pin has travelled along the fold without ripping the handkerchief. This trick will only work if your actions are swift and decisive. If you are too slow pulling the pin down or pushing it up again, you will end up with nothing more than a ruined handkerchief.

Holding Your Drink

Skill Level: ⑧

YOU WILL NEED:
A GLASS OF WATER, A POSTCARD

Whilst this is a relatively straightforward trick in that there is no complicated procedure, it is by no means an easy one to perfect. You need a smooth-rimmed glass and a piece of smooth card – ideally a postcard. Fill the glass to the top with water and wet the rim slightly. Then place the card on top of the glass. Holding the card firmly in place, turn the glass over and take your hand away from the card. By the laws of science, the water should stay in the glass because the pushing power of air against the card is greater than the downward force of the water. But even science has its off days so, to be on the safe side, perform the trick over a sink or a bath.

Jumping Paperclips

 **Skill Level:** ❽

YOU WILL NEED:
A BANKNOTE, TWO PAPERCLIPS

This one will drive you to distraction. By the time you have perfected it, Boyzone will have bus passes, Coronation Street will have become a multi-storey car park and Manchester City will have won the Premiership. In principle, it's easy enough. You take a banknote and bend it into an S-shape, linking the first and second layers with one paper clip and the second and third layers with the other clip. When in place, the clips should be just over an inch apart. In one rapid movement, pull the two ends of the banknote and the clips should link together. But don't bet on it…

Escapology

 **Skill Level: ⑨**

YOU WILL NEED:
A LENGTH OF ROPE, A LARGE HANDKERCHIEF, A TOWEL

There are some things you simply can't escape – like Cliff Richard at Christmas, hosepipe bans at the first hint of summer and Otis the Aardvark all the year round – but this trick is something you can escape from, as budding Houdinis and bondage freaks will testify. You need someone to tie your wrists tightly together with a handkerchief large enough to cater for Cyrano de Bergerac's nose. If you can't find anything of adequate size, a scarf will do. As your wrists are tied, you must keep your fists clenched. Ask your assistant to wind a length of rope over and under the handkerchief and between your wrists and to pull the ends tight. At this point you explain that you will free yourself from the shackles of the rope without removing the handkerchief which is binding your wrists. Ask for a towel to be draped over your wrists so that you can perform your escape without giving the game away. An air of mystique always makes a performance more impressive. With your assistant still holding the ends of the rope tightly, open your fists and extend your fingers. Step back and pull hard on the rope until you are able to trap the loop in the rope between the heels of your hands. Rub your wrists together and step forward to slacken the rope. Continue rubbing your wrists together until you make the loop large enough to slip the fingers of one hand through. Step back quickly to stiffen the rope, manoeuvre the loop over your fingers and wrist and pull it from under the handkerchief. A quick tug and you are free from the rope. Ask for the towel covering your hands to be removed and everyone will see that your wrists are still constrained by the handkerchief.

Restored Rope

Skill Level: ⑨

YOU WILL NEED:
A LENGTH OF STRING OR ROPE, SCISSORS

As illusions go, this may not exactly be on a par with making the Statue of Liberty disappear, but the effect by which a cut piece of string appears to be magically restored is impressive enough. It also has the advantage of being one of those rare classic illusions which you can perform in your own home without having to demolish most of the lounge. Another plus factor is that no preparation is required so the whole routine can be acted out in front of your eagle-eyed friends. When professional magicians perform this trick, they use a length of rope, but for your purposes, string will do nicely.

Take a piece of string, about 3ft long, and tie the ends together in a knot. Take the two ends of the resultant loop in your hands, draping the string between your respective thumbs and forefingers and keeping your palms face upwards. Position the knot so that is an inch below your left forefinger. Twist your right hand, still holding one loop, over towards your body and bring your left hand (still holding the other loop) in front of your right hand. As you do so, turn your left hand so that the two palms are facing each other and slip the loop held by your right hand over the fingers of your left hand. All the string is now in your left hand and has formed a double loop (see illustration). Close your left hand over the string and, with your right hand, move the string until between your left thumb and forefinger you are able to feel the twist in the string which creates the double loop. Hold that twist in position with your left thumb and forefinger, keeping it concealed from the audience, and keeping the knot just below your left forefinger. Ask one of your friends to cut the two strands about an inch above your left thumb and show everyone the two ends of each piece to prove that the string has indeed been cut. In fact, however, because the strands are cut just above the twist and knot, the string is not cut in half at all. All that is being cut is one small section of the loop, with the knot in – the rest of the string remains intact. Next tie together the two ends of the short section, held between your left thumb and forefinger, and demonstrate the knot. Hand your volunteer the length of string containing the original knot and ask him to grip it tightly. Take the other end of the string in your left hand and hold the string taut. Now tell everyone that you are going to restore the string in such a way that nobody will be able to see where it had been cut in two. Cover the second knot with your right hand, rub a little and suddenly slide your hand off the string, taking the knot, which should remain hidden under your hand, with you. Since the knot is, in effect, a separate piece of string, it will slide readily off the longer piece. Ask your volunteer to untie the other knot and, while all eyes are on him, you can slip the fake knot into your pocket. With the knot untied, you are able to present a fully restored length of string and with no evidence of any cut.

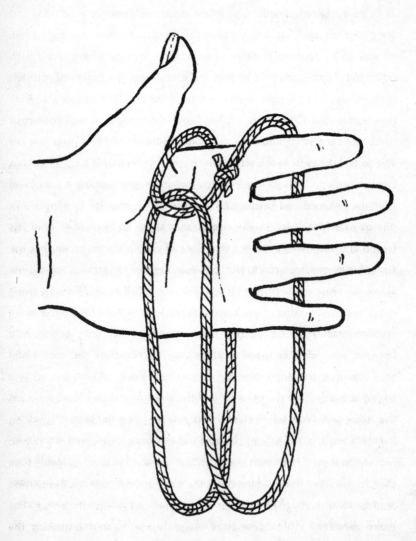

Strip Show

Skill Level: ⑨

YOU WILL NEED:
A CHAIR

The prospect of you removing a girl's clothing for this trick should at least ensure that you have everyone's undivided attention. First you have to find a willing accomplice and make sure she dresses in a manner appropriate to the occasion. This means wearing a loose shirt or blouse which should be buttoned up around the neck, but should otherwise be left to hang loose. She shouldn't put her arms in the sleeves either, merely doing up the button cuffs. Over the shirt she wears a jacket (nothing too tight) so that only the buttoned-up cuffs, the buttoned-up neck and maybe the top two buttons of the shirt are visible underneath. From the outside, it appears that there is nothing peculiar about the way she is dressed. Now for the moment of truth. Request a female volunteer from the audience, saying that you plan to take some of their clothes off. While others hesitate, your volunteer will have been primed to leap forward, declaring that she's game for a laugh. Sit her on a chair, stand behind her and tell everyone that you are going to remove her shirt without taking off her jacket. Gasps of apprehension. Undo the visible buttons at the neck, the front and the cuffs. As the tension reaches fever pitch, grip the collar of the shirt and give it a hefty tug. The entire garment should come away in one piece without disturbing the jacket. Your volunteer will be left to shiver for a few seconds while you acknowledge the rapturous applause. In case of accidents, it is advisable to ask your accomplice to wear a fairly old shirt, rather than risk ripping her favourite top. Of course, this trick can be done by removing the shirt from a man, but it's not as much fun.

Pop the Cork

Skill Level: ⑨

YOU WILL NEED:
A CORK, A BOTTLE, A HANDKERCHIEF

At one time or another, most of us have encountered wine bottle corks which either steadfastly refuse to budge or crumble into tiny fragments. In the latter case, you often have to resort to pushing the cork through the neck and into the actual bottle before draining the precious wine. This trick shows you how to get a cork out from the inside of an empty bottle without smashing the bottle. Unless you're an avid collector of corks, it's a situation which is unlikely to arise, but it's fun anyway. Push the cork through the neck and into the bottle. Then push one end of a handkerchief through the neck (keeping hold of the other end) and toss the contents around until the cork is resting on the handkerchief. Now slowly, but surely, pull the handkerchief out.

In theory, the handkerchief should pull the cork out with it. Then again...

Levitation
For
Beginners

 **Skill Level: ⑩**

YOU WILL NEED:
TWO IDENTICAL PAIRS OF SHOES OR TRAINERS, TWO
STICKS, A LOW TABLE OR BENCH, A SHEET

Are magicians taking the rise when they perform acts of levitation on TV? Certainly they appear phoney, but how on earth do they do it? Well now you can levitate your own friends with this splendid con trick. They might not end up floating around the ceiling, but they will seem to rise a couple of feet off the ground. The key to the trick is acquiring two pairs of identical footwear. This is no easy matter since most discerning folk change their wardrobe from time to time, but you may strike lucky and find a friend with similar taste. If all else fails, there is nothing to stop you using two pairs of identically coloured Wellington boots of similar sizes. There's bound to be a pair in the garden shed tucked under the wheelbarrow and another pair in the garage under a heap of crumpled up paper. The only drawback is that when everyone sees you wearing Wellington boots in your lounge, they'll suspect there's something afoot. Anyway, let's assume you've managed to unearth two pairs of matching trainers. The first thing you need to do is enlist the services of three assistants and let them in on the trick. Bring in an ordinary low table (you can allow people to inspect it if they so desire) which must not only be strong enough to take a person's weight, but must be narrow enough for them to be able to straddle it. The ideal item of equipment is a small bench, but not too many homes possess such a thing. Produce a sheet and instruct two of your assistants to hold it up so that it screens the audience from the table. Get your third helper to lie on the table so that his head is visible at one side of the sheet. At the other side of the sheet, the audience will see what appear to be his shoes sticking out, but in fact they are the matching pair of shoes tied to two long sticks which are resting on the table. For although he is lying down, his knees are bent and his own feet are touching the floor. He is holding the ends of the sticks in his hands. With everything in place, you can start your magic words of levitation, at which the person behind the screen will slowly rise to his feet. He must keep his head back so that it looks as if he is still lying in a horizontal position and, of course, he must remember to raise the dummy shoes in time with his head. As if that isn't enough to remember, he must also keep the sticks level. It's good fun if you can carry it off, but it does need a fair amount of practice, so have a few dummy runs before you go public.

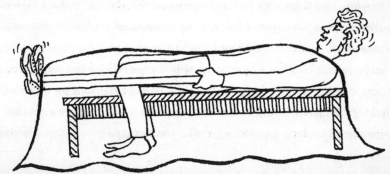

The Daily Pail

 **Skill Level:** ⑩

YOU WILL NEED:
A NEWSPAPER, A SELF-SEAL FOOD BAG, DOUBLE-SIDED
TAPE, GLUE, A JUG OF WATER, A THIN WASHING-UP
SPONGE

This is a trick for the more ambitious performer, someone just the wave of a wand away from sawing acquaintances in half. We've all seen it demonstrated on TV, usually just after the Nigel Lythgoe Dancers and immediately before the scouse comic on one of those summer entertainment shows they used to put out from places like Minehead, Skegness and Bognor Regis, but nevertheless its ability to astound remains undiminished. The trick involves a fair amount of preparation so allow yourself plenty of time. First take a newspaper and glue the pages together along its spine. Open the paper towards the back and, using double-sided tape, fix a self-seal food bag (the sort you keep freezer food in) on to one half of the double-page spread so that the top edge of the bag is in line with the top edge of the page. Stick another piece of tape on the opposite side of the bag, glue along the side and bottom of the page and close the paper so that it is firmly stuck together on every side except the top. Finally open the concealed bag and insert a thin washing-up sponge. With the preparation complete, it is time for the serious business. Show the paper to your audience by opening it at the centre pages and then roll the paper into the shape of a cone. Next put your hand inside the cone and open the top of the bag before slowly pouring in a small jug of water (about 100ml). Your audience (poor gullible fools) think the water is going straight into the newspaper, but you know that it is being poured into the hidden plastic bag where it is soaked up by the sponge. When you have finished pouring the water, unroll the paper from its cone shape and fold it in half again, taking care to close the bag at the same time by running your finger along the top of the page. The deception complete, it is time to open the paper once more at the centre pages to reveal that all the water has vanished. And that's magic...

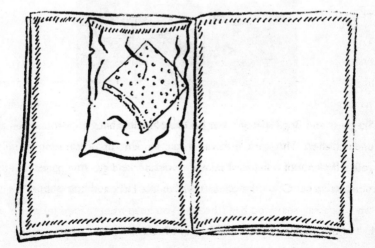

Also published by Carlton Books

Make all your parties go with a bang!

Packed with over 500 party games, *The Best Party Games Book Ever!* will take the worry out of keeping your guests entertained and amused. Available from all good bookshops.

ISBN 1 85868 379 3